THE VIETNAM WAR

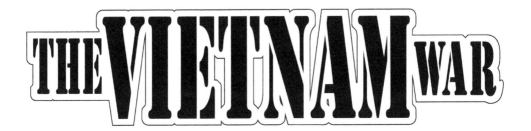

A GRAPHIC HISTORY

WRITTEN BY **DWIGHT ZIMMERMAN**
ART BY **WAYNE VANSANT**

FOREWORD BY GENERAL CHUCK HORNER, USAF (RET.)

A Novel Graphic from Hill and Wang
A division of Farrar, Straus and Giroux
New York

Hill and Wang

A division of Farrar, Straus and Giroux

18 West 18th Street, New York 10011

This is a Z FILE, INC. Book

Text copyright © 2009 by Dwight Jon Zimmerman

Artwork copyright © 2009 by Wayne Vansant

Foreword copyright © 2009 by Chuck Horner

First edition, 2009

Grateful acknowledgment is made for permission to reprint the poem "At the Vietnam Wall" by Duong Tuong, from *Patriots: The Vietnam War Remembered from All Sides* by Christian G. Appy.

Library of Congress Cataloging-in-Publication Data

Zimmerman, Dwight Jon.

    The Vietnam War : a graphic history / written by Dwight Jon Zimmerman ;

  art by Wayne Vansant.-- 1st ed.

     p. cm.

   ISBN-13: 978-0-8090-9495-0 (hardcover : alk. paper)

   ISBN-10: 0-8090-9495-9 (hardcover : alk. paper)

   1. Vietnam War, 1961-1975--Comic books, strips, etc. I. Vansant, Wayne. II. Title.

DS557.7.Z56 2009

959.704'3--dc22

2009007724

Editor: Howard Zimmerman

Design: Zander Cannon and Kevin Cannon

Production Assistant: Elizabeth Maples

www.fsgbooks.com

THIS VOLUME IS DEDICATED TO THE MEMORY OF JOHN GARCIA,
A TALENTED, PASSIONATE, LOVABLE BEAR OF A MAN WHOSE INITIAL VISION
HELPED BRING THE BOOK INTO SHAPE. HE LEFT US FAR TOO SOON.

To my dear friends Sherry and Chuck Jerome,
who were there from the beginning.

--Dwight Jon Zimmerman

To Joe, Jerry, Jim, Joel, Barry, John, Bill,
and others I have known who went to see
the elephant, and came back to tell the tale.

--Wayne Vansant

Dialogue by major historical figures that appears in this volume is taken from actual statements made by the respective individuals or is re-created based on relevant accounts and interviews.

CONTENTS

America's war in Vietnam was so complex it is difficult to understand even today. Like other wars, it began with a premise of good versus bad, and which was which depended on whom you sided with. As the conflict dragged on, these views changed into the reality of a dedicated, committed North Vietnamese enemy and the committed-but-not-dedicated U.S.-led coalition. President Kennedy had committed our nation, but then President Johnson instituted policies that lacked dedication. Finally, President Nixon became dedicated to getting us out of our commitment, at great cost to our honor. Years later, in Desert Storm, our politicians and our military, remembering the lessons of Vietnam, set goals and conducted operations that deserved our unqualified commitment and dedication.

In the case of the Vietnam War, the divergence of political will and goals resulted in constraints on our military operations. Even the most successful air, land, and sea combat could not yield victory. In addition, our South Vietnamese ally's leadership could not rally the dedication of its own people.

Dwight Zimmerman and Wayne Vansant have wrapped their arms around the combat operations and political pressures that shaped our Vietnam War experience—a historian and an artist combining to show, in a clear and comprehensible way, the chain of events that has been described as "the American tragedy." It serves to enlighten those for whom Vietnam is only academic history, so that we may be armed against making the same mistakes in the future. Its narrative voice resonates deeply with those of us who fought that war, who started out idealistic and turned cynical, yet are still proud today of our service.

--General Chuck Horner, USAF (Ret.)

THE VIETNAM WAR

PROLOGUE

"I'VE TOLD THE **AMERICAN PEOPLE**...THAT THIS WILL NOT BE ANOTHER **VIETNAM.**"
                    -- PRESIDENT GEORGE HERBERT WALKER BUSH, 1991

"A LOT OF **PEOPLE** HAVE WARNED PRESIDENT CLINTON THAT BOSNIA WILL TURN INTO ANOTHER **VIETNAM.**"
                    -- BILL MAHER, 1995

"IRAQ IS GEORGE BUSH'S **VIETNAM.**"
    -- SENATOR EDWARD KENNEDY, 2004

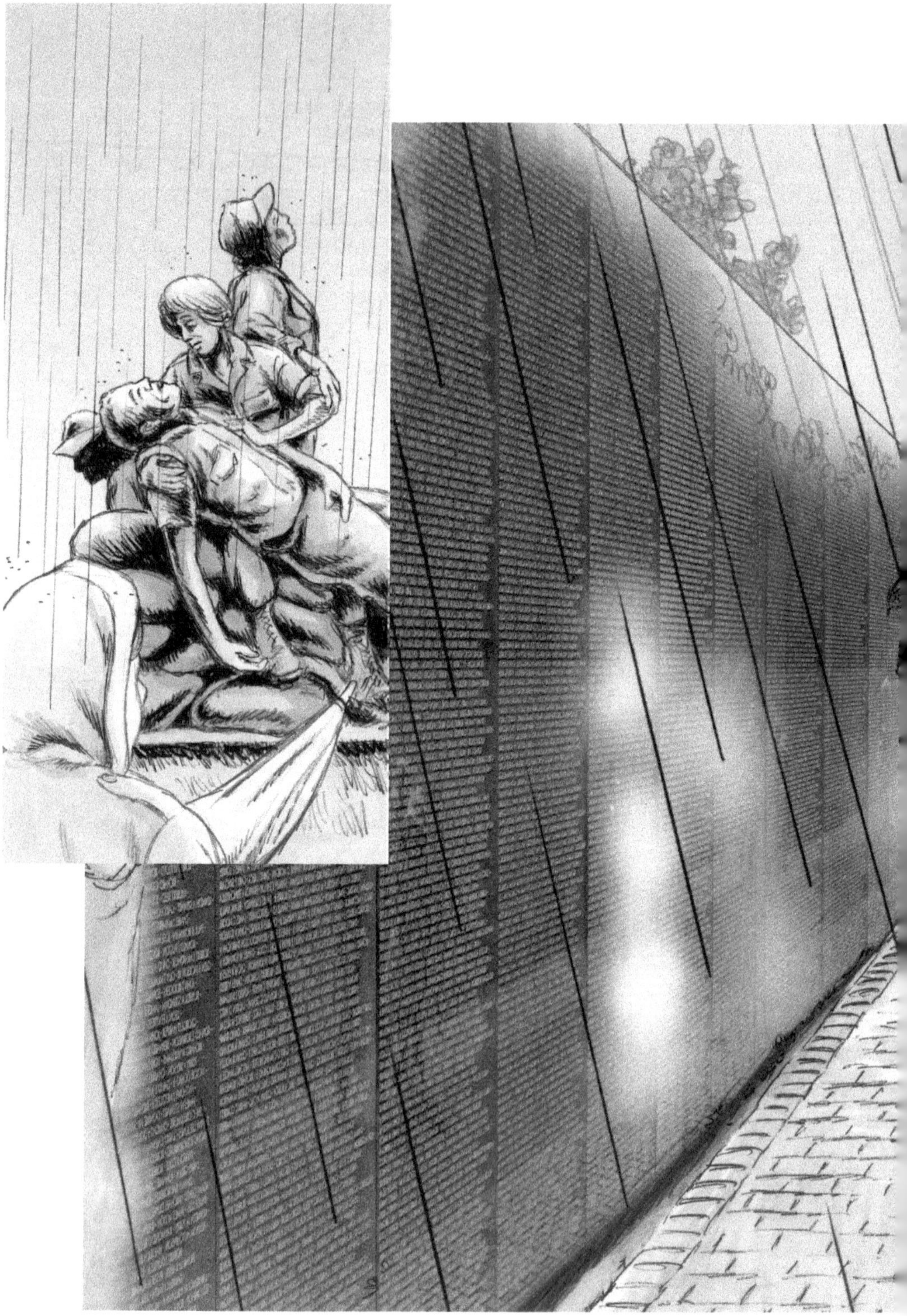

THE **VIETNAM WAR** OFFICIALLY BEGAN ON MARCH 8, 1965, WHEN THE U.S. THIRD MARINE REGIMENT, THIRD MARINE DIVISION, LANDED AT DA NANG, SOUTH VIETNAM.

THE SHOOTING OFFICIALLY STOPPED ON JANUARY 27, 1973, WITH THE SIGNING OF THE **PARIS PEACE ACCORDS.**

BUT THE WAR **TRULY ENDED** ONLY FOR 58,249 MEN AND WOMEN. THEY ARE THE ONES WHOSE NAMES ARE ETCHED IN THE POLISHED BLACK GRANITE PANELS OF THE VIETNAM VETERANS MEMORIAL, KNOWN SIMPLY AS THE **WALL.** FOR THE REST OF AMERICA, THE VIETNAM WAR REMAINED AN OPEN WOUND FOR DECADES. FOR SOME, IT STILL HAS NOT HEALED.

THE WALL BECAME, AND REMAINS, A **PILGRIMAGE SITE** FOR THOSE AFFECTED BY THE CONFLICT. MANY LEAVE MEMENTOS AND **LETTERS** THAT ARE LATER GATHERED AND PRESERVED BY THE NATIONAL PARK SERVICE.

MRS. ELEANOR WIMBISH WAS ONE SUCH VISITOR. IN A LETTER TO HER SON, **WILLIAM R. STOCKS**, SHE WROTE:

Dear Bill,
I came to this black wall again to see and touch your name, and as I do I wonder if anyone ever stops to realize that next to your name, on this black wall, is your mother's heart...

WHAT FOLLOWS IS AN ACCOUNT OF THE **TEN THOUSAND DAYS OF THUNDER** THAT TRAUMATIZED A NATION.

PART ONE:
COMMITMENT

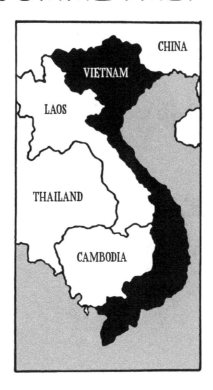

AMERICA'S **COMMITMENT** TO VIETNAM BEGAN IN MAY 1950, WHEN PRESIDENT HARRY TRUMAN AUTHORIZED MODEST MILITARY AND ECONOMIC **AID** TO FRANCE TO HELP IT FIGHT THE COMMUNIST VIETMINH LED BY HO CHI MINH AND TO KEEP ITS COLONIES IN **INDOCHINA**: VIETNAM, LAOS, AND CAMBODIA.

IN 1954, THE **COMMUNIST VICTORY** AT DIEN BIEN PHU ENDED FRENCH COLONIAL RULE IN THE REGION. VIETNAM WAS DIVIDED ROUGHLY AT THE 17TH PARALLEL, CALLED THE DEMILITARIZED ZONE (DMZ), INTO COMMUNIST-LED NORTH AND DEMOCRATIC SOUTH.

BY THEN, THE WORLD WAS LOCKED IN A GLOBAL POWER STRUGGLE CALLED THE **COLD WAR**. ON ONE SIDE WERE THE **COMMUNIST** SOVIET UNION, THE PEOPLE'S REPUBLIC OF CHINA, AND THEIR SATELLITES AND ALLIES. ON THE OTHER SIDE...THE **DEMOCRACIES** OF THE WEST LED BY THE UNITED STATES.

HO CHI MINH WAS DETERMINED TO UNITE VIETNAM--UNDER THE COMMUNIST BANNER, AND UNDER HIS RULE.

TO STOP HIM, **PRESIDENT DWIGHT EISENHOWER** APPROVED AID INCREASES TO SOUTH VIETNAM. IN ADDITION TO ECONOMIC AND MILITARY AID, NUMEROUS POLITICAL **ADVISORS** WERE SENT TO HELP A WEAK GOVERNMENT WHOSE MEMBERS WERE LARGELY INEXPERIENCED.

THE STEADY RISE OF THE COMMUNIST-BACKED **INSURGENCY** IN SOUTH VIETNAM, CALLED THE VIETCONG (VC), PROMPTED PRESIDENT JOHN F. KENNEDY IN 1961 TO SEND 400 SPECIAL FORCES SOLDIERS--**THE GREEN BERETS**-- TO TRAIN THE ARMY OF THE REPUBLIC OF SOUTH VIETNAM (ARVN) IN COUNTERINSURGENCY OPERATIONS.

ON NOVEMBER 22, 1963, PRESIDENT KENNEDY WAS ASSASSINATED AND **VICE PRESIDENT LYNDON JOHNSON** BECAME THE 36TH PRESIDENT OF THE UNITED STATES. THE **PROBLEM** IN VIETNAM WAS NOW HIS...AND IT WAS GROWING.

LYNDON JOHNSON ASKED THE MEMBERS OF HIS PREDECESSOR'S CABINET TO REMAIN AS PART OF HIS **ADMINISTRATION**. IT WAS AN IMPORTANT DISPLAY OF **UNITY** AND CONTINUITY.

JOHNSON, A FORMER SENATOR FROM TEXAS, WAS A **MASTER** OF THE LEGISLATIVE PROCESS AND HAD A KEEN SENSE OF **DOMESTIC ISSUES**. BUT IN MATTERS OF **FOREIGN POLICY**, WHERE HIS HAND WAS LESS SURE, HE WOULD RELY HEAVILY ON THE **ADVICE** OF OTHERS. ONE OF HIS MOST INFLUENTIAL ADVISORS WAS **SECRETARY OF DEFENSE ROBERT S. MCNAMARA**.

MARCH 1964.
THE OVAL OFFICE,
WASHINGTON, D.C.

Mr. President, the situation in South Vietnam has unquestionably been growing worse...

South Vietnam must be free...to accept outside assistance as required to maintain its security...

...Unless we can achieve this objective in South Vietnam, almost all of Southeast Asia will probably fall under Communist dominance...

...Thus, purely in terms of foreign policy, the stakes are high.
Robert S. McNamara
Secretary of Defense
March 16, 1964

CHINA HAD FALLEN UNDER **COMMUNIST CONTROL** IN 1949 DURING THE ADMINISTRATION OF PRESIDENT HARRY TRUMAN, A **DEMOCRAT.** SINCE THEN, THE REPUBLICANS HAD BLAMED THE DEMOCRATS FOR **"LOSING CHINA."**

PROPOSAL FOR A NATIONWIDE WAR ON THE SOURCES OF POVERTY

Special Message to Congress March 16, 1964

FINAL DRAFT

JOHNSON DECIDED VIETNAM COULD NOT "GO THE WAY CHINA WENT." BUT HE ALSO DID NOT WANT TO ASK CONGRESS TO **DECLARE WAR** ON NORTH VIETNAM.

JOHNSON PLANNED AS A **CENTERPIECE** OF HIS ADMINISTRATION A SWEEPING DOMESTIC SOCIAL PROGRAM THAT HE CALLED THE **GREAT SOCIETY.** HE DID NOT WANT A DECLARED WAR TO FOCUS THE NATION'S RESOURCES ON THE OTHER SIDE OF THE WORLD AND SIPHON AWAY THE **FUNDS** HE NEEDED FOR GREAT SOCIETY PROGRAMS.

9

HE BELIEVED HE COULD **CONTAIN** THE CONFLICT IN VIETNAM SO THAT IT WOULD NOT THREATEN HIS GREAT SOCIETY PROGRAM--IF ONLY HE COULD FIND A WAY TO GET CONGRESSIONAL **APPROVAL** SHORT OF A WAR DECLARATION.

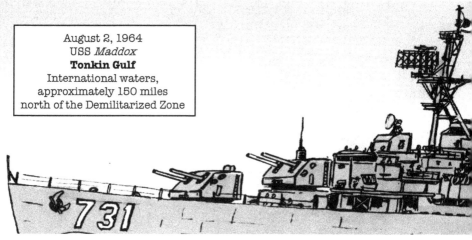

August 2, 1964
USS *Maddox*
Tonkin Gulf
International waters,
approximately 150 miles
north of the Demilitarized Zone

731

AT 4:30 THAT AFTERNOON...

CAPTAIN, WE ARE UNDER **ATTACK** BY NORTH VIETNAMESE PATROL BOATS! ENEMY **TORPEDOES** IN THE WATER!

HARD TO **PORT!**

RETURN FIRE!

THE GREAT SOCIETY

THE GREAT SOCIETY WAS THE MOST SWEEPING **SOCIAL REFORM PROGRAM** SINCE PRESIDENT FRANKLIN ROOSE-VELT'S "NEW DEAL" OF THE 1930S. ITS PRIMARY GOALS WERE THE ELIMINATION OF RACIAL INJUSTICE AND OF POVERTY.

• **CIVIL RIGHTS:** CIVIL RIGHTS ACT OF 1964 (FORBIDDING JOB DISCRIMINATION AND SEGREGATION IN PUBLIC ACCOMMODATIONS); VOTING RIGHTS ACT OF 1965 (VOTING REFORMS); IMMIGRATION AND NATIONALITY SERVICES ACT OF 1965 (ELIMINATING QUOTAS); CIVIL RIGHTS ACT OF 1968 (BANNING HOUSING DISCRIMINATION, EXTENDING CONSTITUTIONAL RIGHTS TO NATIVE AMERICANS).

• **WAR ON POVERTY:** ECONOMIC OPPORTUNITY ACT OF 1964 (FOCUSED ON IMPROVING THE LIFE OF THE POOR THROUGH EDUCATION, JOB TRAINING, AND COMMUNITY DEVELOPMENT).

• **HEALTH CARE:** MEDICARE (1965) AND MEDICAID (1966) WERE CREATED AS A RESULT OF THE SOCIAL SECU-RITY ACT OF 1965.

• **EDUCATION:** ELEMENTARY AND SECONDARY EDUCATION ACT OF 1965 (PROVIDING FOR THE FIRST TIME SIG-NIFICANT FEDERAL AID FOR PUBLIC EDUCATION); HIGHER EDUCATION ACT OF 1965 (GIVING FEDERAL MONIES FOR UNIVERSITIES, STUDENT SCHOLARSHIPS, AND LOW-INTEREST LOANS; AND CREATING THE NATIONAL TEACHER CORPS FOR ECONOMICALLY DISADVANTAGED REGIONS).

FOR SEVERAL WEEKS, THE U.S. NAVY HAD BEEN CONDUCTING **OPERATION DESOTO.**

SPECIALLY EQUIPPED **WARSHIPS** SUCH AS THE DESTROYER *MADDOX* WERE TASKED TO CONDUCT **ELECTRONIC SURVEILLANCE** IN INTERNATIONAL WATERS OFF THE NORTH VIETNAMESE COAST. RISK OF **ATTACK** WAS REGARDED AS LOW.

KA-BAM

• **TRANSPORTATION:** THE DEPARTMENT OF TRANSPORTATION (AUTHORIZED 1966) WAS MADE A CABINET-LEVEL POSITION; URBAN MASS TRANSPORTATION ACT OF 1964.

• **CONSUMER PROTECTION:** CIGARETTE LABELING ACT OF 1965; NATIONAL TRAFFIC AND MOTOR VEHICLE SAFETY ACT OF 1966 AND THE HIGHWAY SAFETY ACT OF 1966 (ESTABLISHING FOR THE FIRST TIME VEHICLE SAFETY STANDARDS); CHILD SAFETY ACT OF 1966 AND FLAMMABLE FABRICS ACT OF 1967; WHOLESOME MEAT ACT OF 1967; TRUTH-IN-LENDING ACT OF 1968, AND OTHER MEASURES.

• **ENVIRONMENTAL PROTECTION:** CLEAN AIR, WATER QUALITY, AND CLEAN WATER RESTORATION ACTS AND AMENDMENTS; WILDERNESS ACT OF 1964; LAND AND WATER CONSERVATION ACT OF 1965; SOLID WASTE DISPOSAL ACT OF 1965; MOTOR VEHICLE AIR POLLUTION CONTROL ACT OF 1965; ENDANGERED SPECIES PRESERVATION ACT OF 1966; NATIONAL TRAILS SYSTEM ACT OF 1968; WILD AND SCENIC RIVERS ACT OF 1968; AIRCRAFT NOISE ABATEMENT ACT OF 1968; AND THE NATIONAL ENVIRONMENTAL POLICY ACT OF 1969.

• **ARTS AND CULTURAL INSTITUTIONS:** NATIONAL FOUNDATION ON THE ARTS AND THE HUMANITIES ACT OF 1965; PUBLIC BROADCASTING ACT OF 1967; CULTURAL CENTERS INCLUDING THE JOHN F. KENNEDY CENTER FOR THE PERFORMING ARTS WERE ESTABLISHED.

ONE NORTH VIETNAMESE **PATROL BOAT** WAS SEVERELY DAMAGED. THE OTHERS WERE DRIVEN OFF BY AIRCRAFT FROM THE CARRIER *TICONDEROGA*.

TWO DAYS LATER, ON THE NIGHT OF **AUGUST 4**, THE *MADDOX* AND SISTER SHIP *TURNER JOY* WERE ONCE AGAIN IN **INTERNATIONAL WATERS** OFF THE NORTH VIETNAMESE COAST, APPROXIMATELY 200 MILES NORTH OF THE DMZ, WHEN THEY REPORTED ANOTHER PATROL BOAT **ATTACK.**

TORPEDOES IN THE WATER!

NEITHER SHIP WAS DAMAGED.

UNDER PRESIDENT JOHNSON'S ORDERS, THE NAVY LAUNCHED **OPERATION PIERCE ARROW** AGAINST THE NORTH VIETNAMESE PETROLEUM STORAGE SITE AT VINH, ABOUT 140 MILES NORTH OF THE DMZ, AND AGAINST NORTH VIETNAMESE NAVAL VESSELS IN THE IMMEDIATE AREA.

THE NAVY FLEW **64 SORTIES** FROM THE AIRCRAFT CARRIERS *CONSTELLATION* AND *TICONDEROGA*. THE PETROLEUM STORAGE SITE WAS **DESTROYED**. A HANDFUL OF VESSELS WERE DAMAGED AND SUNK.

AT THE SAME TIME, SECRETARY OF DEFENSE MCNAMARA WAS PRESENTING TO CONGRESS **"UNEQUIVOCAL PROOF"** OF THE **"UNPROVOKED ATTACKS"** AGAINST AMERICAN WARSHIPS.

MOST PEOPLE **APPROVED** OF JOHNSON'S HANDLING OF THE CRISIS. THE WHITE HOUSE QUICKLY SENT CONGRESS A DRAFT **RESOLUTION** REGARDING SOUTHEAST ASIA. THE **KEY PART** OF THE RESOLUTION WAS SUPPORT FOR THE PRESIDENT IN **REPELLING ARMED ATTACKS** AGAINST U.S. FORCES.

SOME MEMBERS ASKED ABOUT THE PHRASE IN **SECTION 2** THAT AUTHORIZED THE PRESIDENT "TO TAKE ALL NECESSARY STEPS, INCLUDING THE USE OF ARMED FORCE." THEY WERE ASSURED THE ADMINISTRATION HAD NO INTENTION OF **ESCALATING** U.S. INVOLVEMENT.

THE **TONKIN GULF RESOLUTION**, AS IT WAS CALLED, WAS PASSED ON AUGUST 7.

SENATOR WAYNE MORSE, A DEMOCRAT, WAS ONE OF ONLY TWO SENATORS TO VOTE **NO**.

FUTURE GENERATIONS WILL LOOK WITH **DISMAY** AND GREAT DISAPPOINTMENT UPON A CONGRESS...

...WHICH IS NOW ABOUT TO MAKE SUCH AN **HISTORIC MISTAKE**.

EVENTUALLY, **DOCUMENTS** REVEALED A COLLECTION OF MISTAKES AND **FALSE CLAIMS** SURROUNDING THE TONKIN GULF INCIDENTS. BUT, BY THEN, IT WAS FAR **TOO LATE**.

CONGRESS HAD GIVEN PRESIDENT JOHNSON THE POWER TO WAGE **UNDECLARED WAR** IN SOUTH VIETNAM.

1964 WAS A **PRESIDENTIAL ELECTION YEAR.** ALTHOUGH HE NOW HAD ENHANCED AUTHORITY TO WAGE WAR IN SOUTHEAST ASIA, JOHNSON RAN ON A **"PEACE TICKET."**

AT THE TIME, MOST AMERICANS DIDN'T KNOW **ANYTHING** ABOUT VIETNAM, AND JOHNSON WAS CONTENT TO KEEP IT THAT WAY.

ARIZONA **SENATOR BARRY GOLDWATER** WAS THE REPUBLICAN **CANDIDATE.** HE SAID THAT THE UNITED STATES SHOULD EITHER GO ALL-OUT MILITARILY, OR **GET OUT OF SOUTHEAST ASIA.**

GOING ALL-OUT WOULD INCLUDE "CARRYING THE WAR TO NORTH VIETNAM" AND WOULD CONSIDER THE OPTION OF LOW-LEVEL ATOMIC WEAPONS TO DEFOLIATE INFILTRATION ROUTES.

DEMOCRATS LABELED GOLDWATER A **WARMONGER.** THEY AIRED A TV COMMERCIAL IMPLYING THAT IF ELECTED, GOLDWATER WOULD LEAD THE COUNTRY INTO A **NUCLEAR CONFRONTATION.**

JOHNSON **WON,** RECEIVING ABOUT 61 PERCENT OF THE POPULAR VOTE.

IT IS A MANDATE FOR **UNITY,** FOR A GOVERNMENT THAT SERVES NO **SPECIAL** INTEREST.

DESPITE INCREASED **AMERICAN AID** THAT INCLUDED **MILITARY ADVISORS**, BY EARLY 1965 THE **SITUATION** IN SOUTH VIETNAM HAD NOT IMPROVED.

ABOUT 40 PERCENT OF THE COUNTRYSIDE WAS CONTROLLED BY THE VIETCONG. POLITICAL INSTABILITY APPEARED ENTRENCHED.

IT WAS LESS THAN TWO YEARS AFTER THE ASSASSINATION OF PRESIDENT DIEM IN 1963, AND SOUTH VIETNAM WAS ALREADY ON ITS **NINTH GOVERNMENT**--THIS TIME A MILITARY DICTATORSHIP WITH GENERAL NGUYEN CAO KY AS PREMIER AND GENERAL NGUYEN VAN THIEU AS PRESIDENT.

JOHNSON WAS FRUSTRATED. HE REFERRED TO VIETNAM AS "THAT BITCH OF A WAR" THAT DRAINED MONEY FROM "THE WOMAN I LOVE"...THE GREAT SOCIETY PROGRAM.

JOHNSON WANTED A **LOW-COST SOLUTION** TO THE WAR. HIS AIR FORCE CHIEF OF STAFF, GENERAL CURTIS LEMAY, A WORLD WAR II HERO, HAD ONE.

LBJ MET WITH MARTIN LUTHER KING, JR., AND OTHER CIVIL RIGHTS LEADERS, ASSURING THEM OF HIS PRIORITIES.

...AN **ALL-OUT AIR CAMPAIGN.** WE'LL BOMB THE NORTH VIETNAMESE BACK TO THE STONE AGE.

PRESIDENT JOHNSON WAS UNWILLING TO GO THAT FAR. MILITARY ACTION MIGHT CAUSE THE SOVIET UNION AND COMMUNIST CHINA TO SUPPORT NORTH VIETNAM IN FORCE-- AND PRECIPITATE **WORLD WAR III.**

UNLIKE NORTH VIETNAM, WHOSE STATED GOAL WAS A COUNTRY **UNITED** UNDER COMMUNIST RULE, JOHNSON BELIEVED THE PEACEFUL **COEXISTENCE** OF TWO VIETNAMS WAS POSSIBLE.

JOHNSON SOUGHT A MILITARY STRATEGY THAT WAS LIMITED TO USING JUST ENOUGH FORCE TO CONVINCE NORTH VIETNAM TO LEAVE SOUTH VIETNAM ALONE.

SECRETARY OF DEFENSE ROBERT MCNAMARA OFFERED THE **ALTERNATIVE** THE PRESIDENT LIKED.

A FORMER PRESIDENT OF FORD MOTOR COMPANY, MCNAMARA VIEWED THE WAR AS A **BUSINESS MANAGEMENT PROBLEM.**

MCNAMARA AND HIS CIVILIAN SYSTEMS- ANALYST ADVISORS--ALL LACKING FRONT LINE COMBAT EXPERIENCE--CREATED A **LIMITED WAR STRATEGY** OF "GRADUALISM" OR "GRADUATED PRESSURE."

MCNAMARA PROPOSED A PROGRAM OF **STRATEGIC PERSUASION**--THE U.S. WOULD USE AIR STRIKES IN **ESCALATING INCREMENTS** UNTIL HANOI WAS PERSUADED TO STOP ITS SUPPORT OF THE VIETCONG AND AGREE TO NEGOTIATE A PERMANENT **PEACE TREATY**.

THE **TARGETS** WERE BRIDGES, POWER PLANTS, PETROLEUM STORAGE SITES, AND SELECT MILITARY LOCATIONS. MCNAMARA AND HIS ADVISORS WERE CONVINCED HANOI WOULD HAVE TO **CAPITULATE** QUICKLY OR FACE ECONOMIC RUIN.

NORTH VIETNAM WAS HEAVILY **DEPENDENT** ON THE SOVIET UNION AND CHINA FOR MILITARY SUPPLIES AND EQUIPMENT. IT HAD FEWER THAN 17 MILLION PEOPLE, MOST OF WHOM WERE **SUBSISTENCE FARMERS**. ACCORDING TO EVERY STATISTICAL STANDARD...

...NORTH VIETNAM DIDN'T STAND A CHANCE AGAINST THE **MILITARY POWER** OF THE UNITED STATES. THE START DATE FOR THE BOMBING CAMPAIGN WAS **MARCH 2, 1965.**

OPERATION ROLLING THUNDER

THE OPERATION'S CODE NAME WAS **ROLLING THUNDER**. IT WOULD BECOME THE MOST CONTROVERSIAL AIR CAMPAIGN IN AMERICAN HISTORY.

THE FIRST TARGET WAS A SMALL MILITARY SUPPLY DEPOT AND MINOR NAVAL BASE AT QUANG KHE IN NORTH VIETNAM.

AS PART OF ITS "LIMITED WAR" STRATEGY, THE JOHNSON ADMINISTRATION ESTABLISHED NO-BOMBING **"SANCTUAR-IES"** THROUGHOUT NORTH VIETNAM, INCLUDING A **BUFFER ZONE** ALONG THE NORTH VIETNAM-CHINA BORDER. ONCE HANOI LEARNED ABOUT THESE SANCTUARIES, IT MOVED THE BULK OF ITS MILITARY, STRATEGIC BASES, AND INDUSTRIES INTO THEM.

THE NORTH VIETNAMESE GOVERNMENT ALSO SET UP **ANTIAIRCRAFT DEFENSES** WITHIN THE SANCTUARIES. AMERICAN PLANES COULD BE SHOT DOWN WITHOUT FEAR OF REPRISAL.

THE BOMBING CAMPAIGN LASTED FOR **43 MONTHS.** BY THE TIME IT WAS OVER, MORE THAN 643,000 TONS OF BOMBS HAD BEEN DROPPED. AMERICAN MILITARY ESTIMATES WERE THAT THE BOMBING **DESTROYED** 65 PERCENT OF NORTH VIETNAM'S PETROLEUM-OIL-LUBRICANT STORAGE AND 60 PERCENT OF ITS POWER-GENERATING CAPACITY.

OF THE 990 U.S. AIR FORCE, NAVY, AND MARINE AIRCRAFT **SHOT DOWN** OVER NORTH VIETNAM, MOST WERE LOST DURING ROLLING THUNDER MISSIONS. DURING THE FIRST 20 MONTHS, MORE THAN 300 PLANES WERE SHOT DOWN. ATTRITION RATES IN SQUADRONS RANGED FROM 50 TO 75 PERCENT.

ROLLING THUNDER NEVER ACHIEVED ITS **STRATEGIC GOAL:** AT NO POINT DURING THE CAMPAIGN DID THE NORTH VIETNAMESE GOVERNMENT REQUEST **PEACE NEGOTIATIONS.**

WHEN ROLLING THUNDER BEGAN, THE ONLY AMERICAN MILITARY **TROOPS** IN SOUTH VIETNAM WERE ADVISORS AND AIR BASE PERSONNEL, LED BY MILITARY ASSISTANCE COMMAND, VIETNAM (MACV) COMMANDER **GENERAL WILLIAM C. WESTMORELAND.**

WESTMORELAND WORRIED THAT THE VIETCONG OR THE NORTH VIETNAMESE ARMY (NVA) WOULD **RETALIATE** AGAINST ROLLING THUNDER BY ATTACKING AMERICAN **AIR BASES** IN THE SOUTH.

HIS DEPUTY, MAJOR GENERAL JOHN THROCKMORTON, MADE AN **INSPECTION** OF THE AIR BASE AT DA NANG, ABOUT 200 MILES SOUTH OF THE DMZ.

HE WAS APPALLED BY THE **LAX SECURITY.**

GENERAL THROCKMORTON RECOMMENDED THAT A **MARINE EXPEDITIONARY BRIGADE** BE DEPLOYED AT DA NANG TO PROTECT THE BASE. GENERAL WESTMORELAND AGREED.

TWO MARINE BATTALIONS, APPROXIMATELY **1,800 MEN**, LANDED ON THE BEACH AT DA NANG. THEIR ORDERS WERE ONLY TO PROVIDE **SECURITY.** BUT BY THE TIME THEY ARRIVED, MARCH 8-9, 1965, THE **TACTICAL SITUATION** HAD CHANGED.

DESPITE SECRETARY MCNAMARA'S **PREDICTION**, HANOI DID NOT "GET THE MESSAGE" FROM ROLLING THUNDER AND CAPITULATE. INSTEAD, IT INCREASED AID AND **ASSISTANCE** TO THE VC.

VC **ATTACKS** THROUGHOUT THE SOUTH **ESCALATED**--INCLUDING, AS GENERAL WESTMORELAND FEARED, ATTACKS ON AMERICAN AIR BASES.

JOHNSON APPROVED AN **INCREASE** IN AMERICAN TROOP DEPLOYMENT AND THE USE OF GROUND TROOPS IN OFFENSIVE OPERATIONS. BY DECEMBER 1965, THERE WOULD BE ALMOST 185,000 AMERICAN **MILITARY PERSONNEL** IN VIETNAM.

21

SOUTH VIETNAM WAS DIVIDED INTO FOUR MILITARY REGIONS CALLED **CORPS TACTICAL ZONES**, OR CTZS. **CTZ I** WAS THE NORTHERNMOST ZONE AND INCLUDED THE DMZ. **CTZ II** WAS ESSENTIALLY THE CENTRAL HIGHLANDS; **CTZ III** COVERED SAIGON AND THE PROVINCES AROUND IT NORTH OF THE MEKONG DELTA. **CTZ IV** WAS THE SOUTHERNMOST PART AND INCLUDED THE MEKONG DELTA.

THE **U.S. MARINE CORPS** WAS RESPONSIBLE FOR MILITARY OPERATIONS IN CTZ I. INTELLIGENCE REPORTED THAT THE 1ST VIETCONG REGIMENT HAD A MAJOR BASE ON THE **VAN TUONG PENINSULA** NOT FAR FROM THE MARINE BASE AT THE SOUTH VIETNAMESE PORT CITY OF CHU LAI.

IN 1965 A VIETCONG DESERTER SAID THAT THE REGIMENT WAS PLANNING TO **ATTACK** THE MARINE BASE. THE MARINE COMMANDER GOT APPROVAL TO LAUNCH A THREE-PRONG **PREEMPTIVE STRIKE**. ORIGINALLY CODE-NAMED OPERATION SAT-ELLITE, DUE TO A CLERICAL ERROR ITS NAME BECAME **OPERATION STARLITE**.

OPERATION STARLITE BEGAN ON AUGUST 18, 1965. FOR THE **FIRST TIME** IN VIETNAM, THE UNITED STATES LAUNCHED A COMBINED SEA, AIR, AND GROUND OFFENSIVE. MARINE UNITS STATIONED INLAND WERE TO DRIVE THE **VIETCONG** TO THE SEA WHERE THEY WOULD BE SMASHED BY A BLOCKING AMPHIBIOUS FORCE.

ORGANIZED IN JUST **THREE DAYS**, THE COMPLEX OPERATION INVOLVING 5,500 MARINES OF THE 9TH MARINE AMPHIBIOUS BRIGADE AND SUPPORTED BY SHIPS FROM THE U.S. NAVY SEVENTH FLEET TOOK THE VIETCONG BY **SURPRISE**.

TWO MARINES, CORPORAL ROBERT E. O'MALLEY AND LANCE CORPORAL JOE C. PAUL, RECEIVED THE **MEDAL OF HONOR** FOR THEIR ACTIONS.

23

THE VIETCONG FOUGHT HARD, BUT THEY WERE **OVERWHELMED.** SIX DAYS LATER, OPERATION STARLITE WAS OVER. THE MARINES LOST 45 MEN. THE VIETCONG SUFFERED 614 KILLED IN ACTION AND AN UNTOLD NUMBER OF WOUNDED.

THE 1ST VIETCONG REGIMENT HAD BEEN **DESTROYED.** THE VIETCONG REALIZED IT DID NOT HAVE THE **FIREPOWER** TO STAGE A PITCHED BATTLE AGAINST THE AMERICANS, AND FROM THAT POINT ON AVOIDED **SET-PIECE BATTLES.**

THE DRAFT

AT VARIOUS TIMES IN ITS HISTORY, THE UNITED STATES GOVERNMENT HAS PASSED TEMPORARY **CONSCRIPTION LAWS** TO SELECT MEN FOR COMPULSORY MILITARY SERVICE. THE LONGEST RUNNING OF THESE WAS THE **SELECTIVE TRAINING AND SERVICE ACT OF 1940,** ENACTED JUST BEFORE AMERICA'S ENTRY INTO WORLD WAR II AND FINALLY EXPIRING IN 1973.

THE SELECTIVE SERVICE SYSTEM, KNOWN AS **"THE DRAFT,"** WAS OPERATED BY ALMOST 4,000 LOCAL DRAFT BOARDS COMPOSED OF UNPAID VOLUNTEERS, USUALLY VETERANS. ALL MALES HAD TO **REGISTER** AT AGE 17 FOR THE DRAFT TO BE CONDUCTED THE FOLLOWING YEAR. THE FIRST **DRAFT LOTTERY DRAWING** SINCE WORLD WAR II WAS HELD ON DECEMBER 1, 1969. EACH DATE OF THE YEAR WAS PRINTED ON A PIECE OF PAPER AND INSERTED INTO A CAPSULE. THE CAPSULES WERE MIXED AND DRAWN RANDOMLY. THE DATE FROM THE FIRST CAPSULE DRAWN WAS DESIGNATED AS NUMBER 1, AND SO ON. IN 1970, YOUNG MEN BETWEEN THE AGES OF 19 AND 22 WHOSE BIRTHDATES WERE

WARS OFTEN CONTAIN **WEAPONS** OR A METHOD OF FIGHTING THAT VISUALLY DEFINE THEM. IN VIETNAM, IT WAS THE **HELICOPTER.** HELICOPTERS GAVE TROOPS MOBILITY AND FIRE POWER SUPPORT ON AN UNPRECEDENTED SCALE.

MORE THAN **20** DIFFERENT TYPES OF HELICOPTERS WERE USED IN VIETNAM.

THE MOST FAMOUS WAS THE BELL UH-1 IROQUOIS, KNOWN AS THE **"HUEY."**

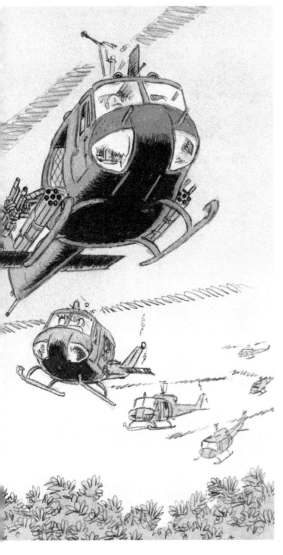

CHOSEN NUMBER 1 THROUGH NUMBER 125 RECEIVED DRAFT NOTICES ORDERING THEM TO REPORT FOR A PHYSICAL AND PROCESSING INTO THE U.S. ARMY. IN 1971, THE HIGHEST LOTTERY NUMBER FOR BEING DRAFTED WAS 95. NO DRAFT ORDERS WERE ISSUED IN 1972.

DEFERMENTS AND **EXEMPTIONS** WERE AVAILABLE FOR COLLEGE STUDENTS, AGRICULTURAL WORKERS, THE DISABLED, AND OTHERS. ANOTHER **OPTION** WAS SERVICE IN THE NATIONAL GUARD OR THE RESERVES, WHICH WAS LESS DEMAND- ING AND DISRUPTIVE. LOCAL DRAFT BOARDS HAD GREAT **DISCRETION** OVER THE GRANTING OF EXEMPTIONS AND DEFERMENTS, AND NUMEROUS CHARGES OF FAVORITISM AND **RACISM** WERE LEVIED DURING THE VIETNAM WAR.

A TOTAL OF **2.7 MILLION SERVICEMEN AND –WOMEN** SERVED IN VIETNAM. THE AVERAGE AGE OF DRAFT-ELIGIBLE MEN IN THE CONFLICT WAS 19, COMPARED TO 26 IN WORLD WAR II. AT THE HEIGHT OF THE WAR, MORE THAN **60 PERCENT** OF THE TROOPS WERE DRAFTEES. PRESIDENT RICHARD NIXON ENDED THE DRAFT IN JANUARY 1973, INAUGURATING THE ALL-VOLUNTEER MILITARY THAT EXISTS TO THIS DAY.

UNDER THE NEW DOCTRINE OF **AIR MOBILITY**, TROOPS WERE NO LONGER
CONFINED TO TRAVEL ON ROADS VULNERABLE TO ROADBLOCKS AND AMBUSH. NOW
THEY COULD RAPIDLY RESPOND TO A **DEVELOPING TACTICAL SITUATION**, DROP
ONTO AN ISOLATED SITE HUNDREDS OF MILES FROM THEIR BASE, ENGAGE THE
ENEMY, AND RETURN WITH CASUALTIES AND ANY PRISONERS BY THE END OF THE DAY.

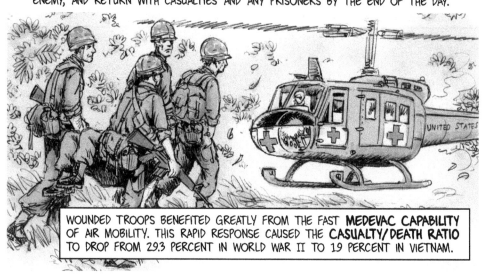

WOUNDED TROOPS BENEFITED GREATLY FROM THE FAST **MEDEVAC CAPABILITY**
OF AIR MOBILITY. THIS RAPID RESPONSE CAUSED THE **CASUALTY/DEATH RATIO**
TO DROP FROM 29.3 PERCENT IN WORLD WAR II TO 19 PERCENT IN VIETNAM.

THOUGH OPERATION STARLITE UTILIZED AIR MOBILITY IN LARGE-
SCALE COMBAT FOR THE **FIRST TIME**, IT WAS STRICTLY IN
COORDINATED SUPPORT OF ADVANCING GROUND TROOPS.

THE FIRST REAL **TEST** OF THE AIR MOBIL-
ITY DOCTRINE WOULD OCCUR THREE MONTHS
LATER IN THE IA DRANG RIVER VALLEY.

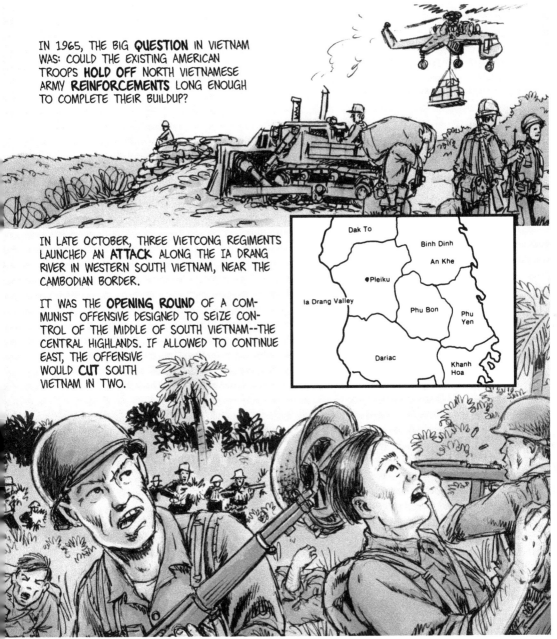

IN 1965, THE BIG **QUESTION** IN VIETNAM WAS: COULD THE EXISTING AMERICAN TROOPS **HOLD OFF** NORTH VIETNAMESE ARMY **REINFORCEMENTS** LONG ENOUGH TO COMPLETE THEIR BUILDUP?

IN LATE OCTOBER, THREE VIETCONG REGIMENTS LAUNCHED AN **ATTACK** ALONG THE IA DRANG RIVER IN WESTERN SOUTH VIETNAM, NEAR THE CAMBODIAN BORDER.

IT WAS THE **OPENING ROUND** OF A COMMUNIST OFFENSIVE DESIGNED TO SEIZE CONTROL OF THE MIDDLE OF SOUTH VIETNAM--THE CENTRAL HIGHLANDS. IF ALLOWED TO CONTINUE EAST, THE OFFENSIVE WOULD **CUT** SOUTH VIETNAM IN TWO.

Dak To
Binh Dinh
An Khe
Pleiku
Ia Drang Valley
Phu Bon
Phu Yen
Dariac
Khanh Hoa

CONVENTIONAL RESPONSE CALLED FOR **LAND-BASED** COUNTERATTACKS ON THE OFFENSIVE'S FLANKS OR FRONT. THIS TIME, DUE TO AIR MOBILITY, THE ATTACK WOULD COME FROM WHERE THE ENEMY WAS MOST VULNERABLE--ITS **REAR**.

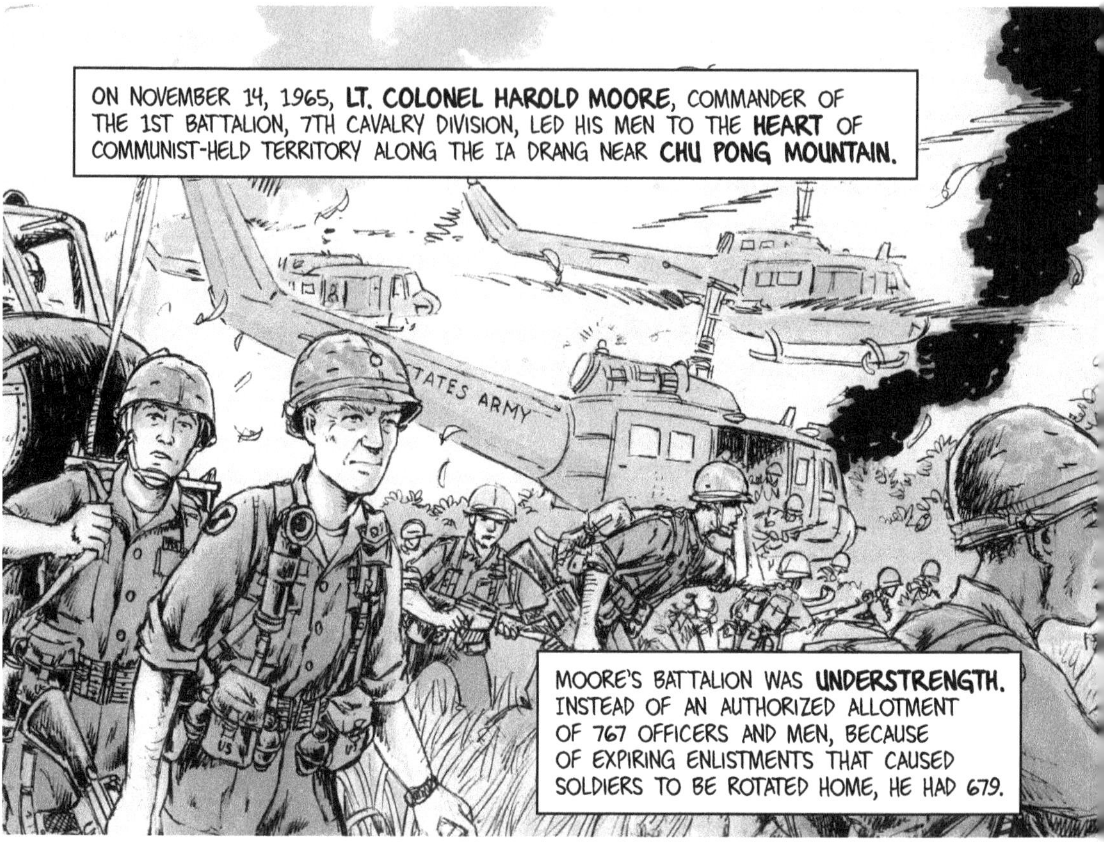
ON NOVEMBER 14, 1965, LT. COLONEL HAROLD MOORE, COMMANDER OF THE 1ST BATTALION, 7TH CAVALRY DIVISION, LED HIS MEN TO THE HEART OF COMMUNIST-HELD TERRITORY ALONG THE IA DRANG NEAR CHU PONG MOUNTAIN.
TATES ARMY
MOORE'S BATTALION WAS UNDERSTRENGTH. INSTEAD OF AN AUTHORIZED ALLOTMENT OF 767 OFFICERS AND MEN, BECAUSE OF EXPIRING ENLISTMENTS THAT CAUSED SOLDIERS TO BE ROTATED HOME, HE HAD 679.

THE FIRST WAVE, ABOUT 160 MEN, ARRIVED AT **LANDING ZONE X-RAY.** WITHIN MINUTES IT CAME UNDER FIRE. THE ATTACK WAS SO FIERCE THE REST OF THE BATTALION COULDN'T LAND.

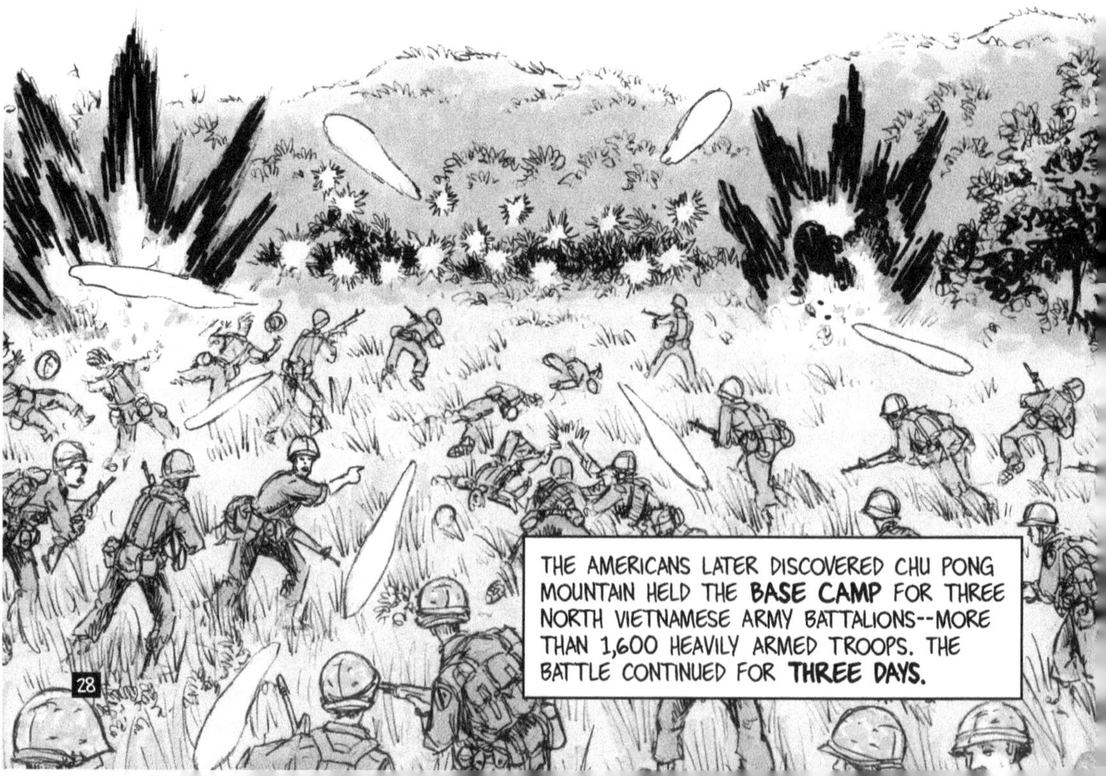
THE AMERICANS LATER DISCOVERED CHU PONG MOUNTAIN HELD THE BASE CAMP FOR THREE NORTH VIETNAMESE ARMY BATTALIONS--MORE THAN 1,600 HEAVILY ARMED TROOPS. THE BATTLE CONTINUED FOR THREE DAYS.

THE AMERICAN TROOPS WERE OUTNUMBERED AND **SURROUNDED.** BUT, THANKS TO THEIR FORWARD AIR CONTROLLERS--**FACS**--THEY WERE NOT ISOLATED AND ALONE. FACS WERE EXPERIENCED FIGHTER PILOTS ASSIGNED TO MAJOR GROUND UNITS. THEY DESIGNATED AND DIRECTED **AIR STRIKES** AGAINST ATTACKING ENEMY UNITS.

THESE AIR STRIKES, ALONG WITH **CANNON FIRE** FROM THE 1ST BATTALION, 21ST ARTILLERY AT LANDING ZONE FALCON, ABOUT FIVE MILES AWAY, PROVIDED MOORE'S MEN AROUND-THE-CLOCK **SUPPORT** AGAINST ENEMY POSITIONS.

ON NOVEMBER 16, THE NORTH VIETNAMESE ARMY ATTACKS ON LANDING ZONE X-RAY **STOPPED.** THOUGH FIGHTING CONTINUED IN THE REGION FOR ANOTHER 10 DAYS, BY NOVEMBER 26, THE COMMUNISTS' OFFENSIVE IN THE CENTRAL HIGHLANDS WAS **ABANDONED.**

THE NORTH VIETNAMESE ARMY'S (NVA'S) ATTEMPT TO SEIZE THE CENTRAL HIGHLANDS HAD **FAILED**.

BUT THE NORTH VIETNAMESE **LEADERSHIP** HAD LEARNED THE AMERICAN WAY OF WAGING WAR AND HAD TAKEN FROM THE CAMPAIGN A CRUCIAL **STRATEGIC LESSON** ABOUT AMERICAN TROOPS AND THEIR SUPERIOR FIREPOWER AND TECHNOLOGY.

AIR MOBILITY TACTICS HAD TAKEN THEM BY **SURPRISE**. THE COMMUNISTS' EXPERIENCE IN FIGHTING THE MUCH WEAKER FRENCH, THEIR FORMER COLONIAL MASTERS, HAD NOT PREPARED THEM FOR THE MASSIVE AND SUSTAINED AIR AND ARTILLERY **COUNTERMEASURES** OF THE AMERICANS. THE GROWING AMERICAN PRESENCE PROVOKED A **CRISIS** AMONG THE RULING POLITBURO OF NORTH VIETNAM ON HOW THE WAR SHOULD BE CONTINUED--OR, EVEN, **IF** IT SHOULD BE CONTINUED.

PART TWO:
THE LIGHT AT THE END OF THE TUNNEL

THE **"DOMINO EFFECT"** WAS THE POLITICAL THEORY USED BY MANY TO JUSTIFY THE STEADY TROOP BUILDUP AND INCREASING COMBAT ACTION IN SOUTHEAST ASIA. THE BELIEF WAS THAT IF SOUTH VIETNAM FELL TO THE COMMUNISTS, **OTHER NATIONS** IN THE REGION, INCLUDING CAMBODIA, THAILAND, BURMA, MALAYSIA, AND INDONESIA, WOULD **FALL** AS WELL, LIKE A ROW OF DOMINOES.

THE U.S. DRAFT AND INCREASING **TROOP DEPLOYMENT** NOW MEANT THAT MORE AND MORE YOUNG MEN FRESHLY GRADUATED FROM HIGH SCHOOL FACED A **SOBERING REALITY:** THEY STOOD A GOOD CHANCE OF BEING FORCED TO SERVE AND FACE **COMBAT.** IN THE YEARS BETWEEN THE END OF THE KOREAN WAR AND THE START OF THE VIETNAM WAR, THE DRAFT AFFECTED RELATIVELY FEW YOUNG MEN. THE VIETNAM WAR CHANGED THAT. NOW HUNDREDS OF THOUSANDS OF YOUNG MEN FOUND THAT THEY STOOD A VERY GOOD CHANCE OF BEING SENT OFF TO **FIGHT** IN A WAR ON THE OTHER SIDE OF THE WORLD FOR REASONS THAT MANY THOUGHT WERE UNCLEAR AND INCREASINGLY UNJUSTIFIABLE.

THE GROWING SENSE OF **FRUSTRATION** OVER THE ELUSIVENESS OF VICTORY IN VIETNAM CAUSED AN INCREASING NUMBER OF AMERICAN CITIZENS FROM ALL WALKS OF LIFE TO ASK A SIMPLE AND TROUBLING QUESTION: **"WHY?"**

RECENT MILITARY **DEFEATS** REVIVED LONG-STANDING **RIVALRIES** IN THE NORTH VIETNAMESE POLITBURO. DURING POLICY DEBATES, THE QUESTION OF WHETHER OR NOT TO CONTINUE THE WAR WAS RAISED. THAT POINT WAS SETTLED WHEN HO CHI MINH SAID IT **WOULD.** THE **DEBATE** THEN FOCUSED ON **HOW.**

ON ONE SIDE WAS SENIOR GENERAL **NGUYEN CHI THANH**, COMMANDER OF NORTH VIETNAMESE ARMY FORCES IN THE SOUTH, AND HIS ALLY LE DUAN, SECRETARY GENERAL OF THE COMMUNIST PARTY IN VIETNAM. THANH BELIEVED THE HEAVY CASUALTIES THE AMERICANS WOULD SUFFER--IN HIS WORDS, THE "COFFINS GOING HOME"--WOULD QUICKLY MAKE THEM QUIT.

NGUYEN CHI THANH

OPPOSING THEM WERE MINISTER OF DEFENSE AND SENIOR GENERAL **VO NGUYEN GIAP** AND HIS MAIN ALLY, TRUONG CHINH, THE THIRD MOST POWERFUL MEMBER OF THE POLITBURO. GIAP REMAINED A GUERILLA-WARFARE ADVOCATE--CONVINCED THAT THE NVA AND VIETCONG UNITS COULD NEVER DEFEAT THE AMERICAN FORCES CONVENTIONALLY WITHOUT SUFFERING UNACCEPTABLY HIGH CASUALTIES.

THANH'S ARGUMENT CARRIED THE DAY--BEGINNING IN NOVEMBER 1965 THE COMMUNIST STRATEGY WOULD BE TO **"BAIT"** AMERICAN UNITS INTO ACTION IN REMOTE SECTIONS AND THEN **ANNIHILATE** THEM WITH LOCALLY SUPERIOR FORCES.

VO NGUYEN GIAP

GENERAL WESTMORELAND WAS ALSO WRESTLING WITH HOW TO CONTINUE THE FIGHT IN VIETNAM. ANY GROUND OPERATIONS OUTSIDE SOUTH VIETNAM'S BORDERS WERE FORBIDDEN. THIS MEANT NORTH VIETNAM, THE COMMUNIST BASE CAMPS, AND THE HO CHI MINH TRAIL SUPPLY ROUTE IN LAOS AND CAMBODIA COULD BE HIT ONLY BY **AIR STRIKES** PERSONALLY APPROVED BY PRESIDENT JOHNSON.

THIS **RESTRICTION** PREVENTED WESTMORE-LAND FROM CARRYING AN ATTACK NEAR THE BORDER TO ITS PROPER CONCLUSION--THE **DESTRUCTION** OF ENEMY UNITS. ONCE HARRIED ENEMY UNITS CROSSED THE BORDER, THEY COULD REST AND RECOVER FREE FROM **REPRISALS.**

STILL, WESTMORELAND WAS NOT WITHOUT RESOURCES. HE HAD AN IMPORTANT UNCONVENTIONAL-WARFARE TOOL ALREADY IN PLACE: SPECIAL FORCES--**THE GREEN BERETS.**

THEY ORGANIZED THE **MONTAGNARDS,** A TRIBE ETHNICALLY DISTINCT FROM THE VIETNAMESE THAT LIVED IN THE CENTRAL HIGHLANDS, INTO EFFECTIVE ANTICOMMUNIST **PARAMILITARY FIGHTERS** CALLED CIVILIAN IRREGULAR DEFENSE GROUPS, OR CIDGs.

SEPARATELY, THE MA-
RINES IN THE CORPS
TACTICAL ZONE I CRE-
ATED THE **COMBINED
ACTION PLATOON
(CAP)** PROGRAM
TO HELP VILLAGERS
RESIST THE VIETCONG.
SQUADS OF MARINES--
12 MEN OR FEWER--
WOULD BE STATIONED
IN HAMLETS WHERE
THEY WOULD LIVE
SIDE BY SIDE WITH
THE VILLAGERS.

THEY GOT TO KNOW
VILLAGERS AS
INDIVIDUALS, AND WHEN
NOT ON PATROL OR
HELPING IN DEFENSE
ISSUES, ASSISTED ON
LOCAL **CIVIC** AND
HEALTH PROJECTS.
CAPS WOULD PROVE
EFFECTIVE IN DENYING
THE VIETCONG
SUPPORT AMONG THE
RURAL POPULATION.

BUT WESTMORELAND WAS A **"BIG ARMY,"** CONVENTIONAL-WARFARE GENERAL WHO
REGARDED THE SPECIAL FORCES AND MARINES' EFFORTS AS **SIDESHOWS** TO THE
REAL FIGHT. HIS PRIMARY PLAN WOULD USE LARGE UNITS AND OVERWHELMING
FIREPOWER IN **"SEARCH-AND-DESTROY"** EFFORTS
TO HUNT, CORNER, AND ELIMINATE A GUERILLA
ENEMY AND ITS HIDDEN BASES.

THANKS TO PRESIDENT JOHNSON, WESTMORELAND NOW HAD HELP
FROM OTHER NATIONS--PARTICULARLY TROOPS FROM SOUTH
KOREA, AUSTRALIA, AND NEW ZEALAND. HE WOULD SOON USE THEM.

WESTMORELAND'S OFFENSIVE BEGAN ON JANUARY 8, 1966, WITH **OPERATION CRIMP.** IT INVOLVED ALMOST 8,000 TROOPS, THE LARGEST DEPLOYMENT TO DATE. ITS PURPOSE WAS TO FIND AND DESTROY THE VIETCONG HEADQUARTERS IN THE COMMUNIST STRONGHOLD, KNOWN AS THE **IRON TRIANGLE,** NORTH OF SAIGON.

THE OPERATION ENDED SIX DAYS LATER. THE TROOPS HAD DISCOVERED A SOPHISTICATED **TUNNEL SYSTEM,** BUT DID NOT FIND THE HEADQUARTERS.

THE AMERICANS HAD BETTER LUCK LATER WITH **OPERATION VAN BUREN.** THE COMBINED U.S., SOUTH KOREAN, AND SOUTH VIETNAMESE ATTACK WAS LAUNCHED ON JANUARY 19, 1966. ITS OBJECTIVE WAS THE DESTRUCTION OF THE NVA 95TH REGIMENT BEFORE IT COULD CONFISCATE THE RICH **RICE HARVEST** FROM SOUTH VIETNAM'S TUY HOA VALLEY.

THE COMMUNISTS LOST SO MANY TROOPS THAT THEY REQUESTED, AND RECEIVED, A **TEMPORARY CEASE-FIRE** FROM JANUARY 20 TO 23, OSTENSIBLY TO HONOR **TET,** THE LUNAR NEW YEAR.

35

THE CEASE-FIRE ENDED DRAMATICALLY WITH THE LAUNCHING ON JANUARY 24TH OF **OPERATION MASHER** (LATER CHANGED TO **WHITE WING**), A 42-DAY SEARCH-AND-DESTROY MISSION CONDUCTED OVER 2,000 SQUARE MILES IN CTZs I AND II OF UPPER SOUTH VIETNAM.

COMBINED AMERICAN, SOUTH KOREAN, AND SOUTH VIETNAMESE UNITS **MAULED** TWO VIETCONG AND TWO NORTH VIETNAMESE REGIMENTS. BUT THEIR **SUCCESS** IN FREEING APPROXIMATELY 140,000 SOUTH VIETNAMESE FROM COMMUNIST DOMINANCE PROVED **SHORT-LIVED**, BECAUSE ONLY LIMITED FOLLOW-UP PACIFICATION EFFORTS WERE IMPLEMENTED. THOUGH THE AMERICANS HAD "CLEARED" THE AREA, THEY COULD NOT **HOLD** IT.

SECRETARY OF DEFENSE ROBERT STRANGE MCNAMARA

MCNAMARA WAS PRESIDENT OF THE FORD MOTOR COMPANY WHEN HE BECAME SECRETARY OF DEFENSE IN THE KENNEDY ADMINISTRATION IN 1961. MCNAMARA IMPOSED A NUMBER OF PRACTICES THAT HE AND HIS ADVISORS, KNOWN AS THE "WHIZ KIDS," HAD HONED IN THE BUSINESS WORLD, THE MOST FAMOUS BEING A **STATISTICAL CONTROL ANALYSIS SYSTEM**, WHICH, AMONG OTHER THINGS, ESTABLISHED GUIDELINES TO EVALUATE AND JUSTIFY PROCUREMENT COSTS. IN EFFECT, MCNAMARA BELIEVED THAT A WAR SHOULD BE RUN LIKE A **CORPORATION**. AT TIMES, MCNAMARA MICROMANAGED AMERICAN EFFORTS IN VIETNAM DOWN TO OPERATIONAL LEVELS--NORMALLY THE RESPONSIBILITY OF JUNIOR OFFICERS. AS A RESULT, HE BECAME BOGGED DOWN AND LATER **OVERWHELMED** TO THE POINT WHERE HE WAS UNABLE TO PERFORM THE PROPER POLICY-MAKING FUNCTION OF HIS POSITION. MCNAMARA PRIVATELY BEGAN TO HAVE DOUBTS ABOUT A SUCCESSFUL MILITARY SOLUTION TO THE WAR AS EARLY AS 1965. THESE **DOUBTS** BECAME SO PRONOUNCED THAT RUMORS OF THEM BEGAN TO SURFACE PUBLICLY IN 1967. MCNAMARA LEFT OFFICE ON FEBRUARY 29, 1968. REGARDLESS, JOHNSON AWARDED MCNAMARA THE **MEDAL OF FREEDOM**, THE NATION'S HIGHEST CIVILIAN AWARD, AND THE DISTINGUISHED SERVICE MEDAL, AND APPOINTED HIM TO BE PRESIDENT OF THE WORLD BANK. MCNAMARA RETIRED FROM THE WORLD BANK IN 1981.

MEANWHILE, SECRETARY OF DEFENSE ROBERT MCNAMARA, OBSESSED WITH TRYING TO **QUANTIFY** AMERICAN GOALS AND ESTABLISH STATISTICAL **BENCHMARKS**, PREPARED A FORMAL **MEMORANDUM** FOR GENERAL WEST-MORELAND THAT SET FORTH SIX GOALS FOR THE U.S. EFFORT IN SOUTH VIETNAM.

INTENDED TO APPLY TO 1966, WHEN THE UNITED STATES WOULD HAVE MORE THAN 385,000 TROOPS IN SOUTH VIETNAM, IT SERVED AS A **GUIDELINE** FOR THE NEXT THREE YEARS AS WELL.

GENERAL WILLIAM CHILDS WESTMORELAND

FOR GOOD AND ILL, WESTMORELAND BECAME THE **FACE** OF AMERICA'S DEFEAT IN THE VIETNAM WAR. GENERAL WEST-MORELAND BECAME COMMANDER, MILITARY ASSISTANCE COMMAND, VIETNAM, ON JUNE 20, 1964. THOUGH GENERAL WESTMORELAND WAS THE COMMANDER OF AMERICAN FORCES IN SOUTH VIETNAM, HE WAS NOT THE **COUNTERPART** OF NORTH VIETNAMESE COMMANDER GENERAL VO NGUYEN GIAP, WITH WHOM HE HAS BEEN COMPARED. GIAP WAS ALSO A SENIOR MEMBER OF THE GOVERNMENT AND ITS MINISTER OF DEFENSE, AND AS SUCH POSSESSED RESPONSIBILI-TIES THAT, IN THE UNITED STATES, WERE DIVIDED AMONG SIX INDIVIDUALS, INCLUDING WESTMORELAND, SECRETARY OF DEFENSE MCNAMARA, AND CHAIRMAN OF THE JOINT CHIEFS OF STAFF GENERAL EARLE WHEELER. THOUGH WEST-MORELAND COULD NOT DEVELOP THE **WAR STRATEGY** FOR VIETNAM AND ALLOCATE THE TROOPS AND RESOURCES TO EXECUTE IT, HE WAS RESPONSIBLE FOR HOW THE TROOPS AND MATÉRIEL WOULD BE USED ONCE THEY ARRIVED IN SOUTH VIETNAM. WESTMORELAND FOCUSED ON DEVELOPING A MASSIVE **MILITARY RESPONSE** TO THE GROWING ENEMY THREAT AND LARGELY IGNORED THE PACIFICATION PROGRAM--KNOWN AS THE **"OTHER WAR"**--TO WIN THE SUPPORT OF THE RURAL CIVILIAN POPULATION. WESTMORELAND LEFT MACV IN 1968 TO ASSUME DUTIES AS ARMY CHIEF OF STAFF IN WASHINGTON. HE RETIRED IN 1972 AND DIED IN 2005.

1. Attrit, by year's end, VietCong and North Vietnamese forces at a rate as high as their capability to put men into the field.

2. Increase the percentage of VC and NVA base areas denied the VC from 10-20 percent to 40-50 percent.

3. Increase the critical (important) roads and railroads open for use from 30 to 50 percent.

4. Increase the population in secure areas from 50 to 60 percent.

5. Pacify the four selected high-priority areas, increasing the pacified population by 235,000.

6. Insure the defense of all military bases, political population centers, and food-producing areas now under government control.

BODY COUNT

BODY COUNTS WERE A DIRECT RESULT OF SECRETARY OF DEFENSE ROBERT MCNAMARA'S ATTEMPT TO ESTABLISH A MEASURE OF **PROGRESS** IN THE VIETNAM WAR. THOUGH THE POLICY BECAME A SUBJECT OF CONTROVERSY THAT FURTHER **ERODED** AMERICAN CIVILIAN SUPPORT FOR THE WAR, THERE WAS HISTORICAL **PRECEDENT** TO UPHOLD THIS STRATEGY OF ATTRITION.

BODY COUNTING INEVITABLY LED TO ABUSES SUCH AS **INFLATED REPORTS.** BUT ULTIMATELY, THE ESTIMATED TOTAL OF COMMUNIST BATTLE DEATHS IN THE VIETNAM WAR OF BETWEEN 500,000 AND 600,000 TROOPS CAME TO BE REGARDED AS **ACCURATE.** GENERAL GIAP WENT ON RECORD A NUMBER OF TIMES STATING HALF A MILLION OF HIS MEN HAD BEEN LOST. THIS MEANT THAT NORTH VIETNAM LOST BETWEEN 2.5 AND 3 PERCENT OF ITS PREWAR POPULATION. IN HIS ARTICLE "THE SEARCH FOR THE 'BREAKING POINT' IN VIETNAM," JOHN E. MUELLER WROTE THAT THIS ALSO MEANT "THE MILITARY COSTS ACCEPTED BY THE COMMUNISTS IN VIETNAM WERE VIRTUALLY UNPRECEDENTED HISTORICALLY."*

IN THEIR BOOK *THE WAGES OF WAR, 1816-1965,* PUBLISHED IN 1972, J. DAVID SINGER AND MELVIN SMALL STUDIED 100 INTERNATIONAL WARS. ONE OF THE MOST **TELLING STATISTICS** WAS THAT ONLY IN A HANDFUL OF

GENERAL WESTMORELAND WAS IN EFFECT BEING TREATED LIKE A **CORPORATE EXECUTIVE** CHARGED WITH MEETING QUARTERLY SALES AND MARKET-SHARE GOALS. THIS MEMORANDUM WOULD INSPIRE ONE OF THE MOST **CONTROVERSIAL BENCHMARKS** OF THE VIETNAM WAR...THE **BODY COUNT.**

SINCE WESTMORELAND COULD NOT ACHIEVE VICTORY IN THE TRADITIONAL WAY BY **INVADING** NORTH VIETNAM...

...HE TURNED TO THE DESTRUCTION OF ENEMY FORCES--A WAR OF **ATTRITION**--AS HIS INDICATOR OF VICTORY.

THESE CONFLICTS DID THE PARTICIPANTS LOSE AS MUCH AS 2 PERCENT OF THEIR PREWAR POPULATIONS IN **BATTLE DEATHS** OF COMBATANTS. IN WORLD WAR II, FOR INSTANCE, GERMANY AND THE SOVIET UNION LOST 4.4 PERCENT. JAPAN LOST 1.4 PERCENT, AND THE UNITED STATES LOST 0.3 PERCENT.

BODY COUNTS ARGUABLY BECAME THE MOST VISIBLE EXAMPLE OF A **FLAWED AMERICAN STRATEGY.** WHEREAS THE UNITED STATES BELIEVED IT WAS INVOLVED IN A CONFLICT MEASURABLE IN TROOPS AND INDUSTRIAL CAPACITY ENGAGED AND DESTROYED, THE VIETNAMESE COMMUNIST LEADERSHIP FOUGHT AN **IDEOLOGICAL WAR** WITH STRATEGIES THEY CONTINUOUSLY REFINED.

THE GULF OF THIS **MISPERCEPTION** IS SUMMARIZED IN THE FOLLOWING QUOTES. HO CHI MINH SAID IN 1966, "IF [AMERICANS] WANT TO MAKE WAR FOR **20 YEARS,** THEN WE SHALL MAKE WAR FOR 20 YEARS." AN ANONYMOUS NORTH VIETNAMESE LIEUTENANT-COLONEL SAID OF THE WAR, "I MAY NOT SEE THE END MYSELF. BUT I EXPECT MY **CHILDREN** WILL." AFTER THE WAR, IN 1976, GENERAL WESTMORELAND NOTED, "ANY AMERICAN COMMANDER WHO TOOK THE SAME VAST LOSSES AS GENERAL GIAP WOULD HAVE BEEN SACKED OVERNIGHT."

* *INTERNATIONAL STUDIES QUARTERLY,* DECEMBER 1980.

WESTMORELAND'S GOAL WAS TO REACH THE **"CROSSOVER POINT,"** WHERE THE NUMBER OF ENEMY CASUALTIES BECAME GREATER THAN THE COMMUNISTS' ABILITY TO **REPLACE** THEM. IN OTHER WORDS, BLEED THE ENEMY TO DEATH.

TO PROVE THE STRATEGY'S **EFFECTIVENESS**, HE HAD TO HAVE HIS MEN COUNT THE DEAD ENEMY BODIES.

EACH DAY WESTMORELAND'S HEADQUARTERS RELEASED ITS **TALLY** OF ENEMY CASUALTIES.

THE **PENTAGON** REPORTS TODAY THAT THE ENEMY SUFFERED...

THE JOHNSON ADMINISTRATION ASSURED AMERICANS THAT THE RISING BODY-COUNT TOTAL WOULD SOON REACH A "BREAKING POINT" THAT WOULD FORCE HANOI TO THE **BARGAINING TABLE.**

IN WASHINGTON, HOWEVER, SOME LEGISLATORS WERE BEGINNING TO HAVE **SECOND THOUGHTS** ABOUT THE VIETNAM WAR.

SENATOR J. WILLIAM FULBRIGHT, THE POWERFUL CHAIRMAN OF THE SENATE FOREIGN RELATIONS COMMITTEE, HAD ALREADY TURNED AGAINST THE WAR. IN JUST **ONE YEAR**, 1965, AMERICAN TROOP PRESENCE HAD GONE FROM 23,300 TO 184,300 MEN...

...AND IN JANUARY 1966 PRESIDENT JOHNSON REQUESTED AN **ADDITIONAL** $12.8 BILLION, ALONG WITH ANOTHER 100,000 TROOPS, FOR THE VIETNAM WAR.

HOW MANY **MORE REQUESTS** WOULD BE MADE, AND AT WHAT COST?

IN FEBRUARY 1966, THE **SENATE FOR-EIGN RELATIONS COMMITTEE** VOTED TO HAVE ITS HEARINGS ON THE WAR TELEVISED. IN AN ERA WHEN CBS, NBC, AND ABC WERE THE ONLY NATIONALLY BROADCAST TELEVISION NETWORKS, IT WAS AN **EXTRAORDINARY DECISION.**

THEN, ON MARCH 1, 1966, A BILL TO **REPEAL** THE TONKIN GULF RESOLUTION WAS SPONSORED BY SENATOR WAYNE MORSE, ONE OF THE RESOLUTION'S ORIGINAL **OPPONENTS.** IT WAS VOTED DOWN 95-5, BUT THE ACTION WAS A **PORTENT** OF THINGS TO COME.

IN AN EFFORT TO **DEFUSE** THE SMALL BUT GROWING OPPOSITION TO THE WAR, PRESIDENT JOHNSON CONVENED THE **HONOLULU CONFERENCE** ON FEBRUARY 7-9, 1966.

TOGETHER WITH HIS SENIOR ADVISORS, HE MET THE **LEADERS** OF SOUTH VIETNAM. THE CONFERENCE CONCLUDED WITH THE SOUTH VIETNAMESE PROMISING TO DRAFT A NEW, FAIR **CONSTITUTION** AND ENACT A VARIETY OF **SOCIAL REFORMS** IN RETURN FOR INCREASED MILITARY ASSISTANCE.

SENATOR J. WILLIAM FULBRIGHT

SENATOR JAMES WILLIAM FULBRIGHT OF ARKANSAS, CHAIRMAN OF THE SENATE FOREIGN RELATIONS COMMITTEE, BE-CAME ARGUABLY THE MOST POWERFUL AND PERSISTENT **CRITIC** OF THE VIETNAM WAR. FULBRIGHT WAS ELECTED TO THE HOUSE OF REPRESENTATIVES IN 1942 AND TO THE SENATE IN 1944. HE BECAME A MEMBER OF THE **FOREIGN RELATIONS COMMITTEE** IN 1949 AND WAS ITS CHAIRMAN FROM 1959 TO 1974, THE LONGEST-SERVING CHAIR IN THE COMMITTEE'S HISTORY.

FULBRIGHT INITIALLY SUPPORTED THE WAR AND WAS AN INFLUENTIAL BACKER OF THE **TONKIN GULF RESOLUTION.** THROUGHOUT 1965, HE PUBLICLY SUPPORTED THE PRESIDENT'S POLICIES, WHILE PRIVATELY HIS **DOUBTS** BEGAN TO GROW.

THESE DOUBTS BECAME **PUBLIC** DURING THE TELEVISED FOREIGN RELATIONS COMMITTEE HEARINGS ON AMERICA'S POLICY IN VIETNAM THAT BEGAN IN FEBRUARY 1966. HE ADDED FURTHER FUEL TO THE ANTIWAR FIRE WITH HIS BOOK *THE ARROGANCE* OF POWER, PUBLISHED IN 1966. IN IT HE POINTEDLY **CHALLENGED** THE CONSENSUS IN GOVERN-MENT CIRCLES THAT U.S. MILITARY INTERVENTION IN SOUTHEAST ASIA WAS NECESSITATED BY **COLD WAR GEO-POLITICS.** ACKNOWLEDGING AMERICA'S OWN CIVIL RIGHTS MOVEMENT, HE WROTE, "THERE IS SOMETHING UNSEEMLY ABOUT A NATION CONDUCTING A FOREIGN POLICY THAT INVOLVES IT IN THE AFFAIRS OF MOST OF THE NATIONS

WHILE GENERAL WESTMORELAND RAMPED UP THE LAND WAR, THE **U.S. NAVY** FACED ITS OWN CHALLENGES. IN THE EARLY 1960s, ITS DOCTRINE AND FORCE STRUCTURE WERE DESIGNED TO FIGHT A **NUCLEAR** WAR.

AN ACROSS-THE-BOARD CRASH **REFOCUS-AND-REFIT PROGRAM** ENSUED TO IMPLEMENT THE NAVY'S STRATEGY IN SOUTHEAST ASIA--WHAT IT TERMED A **"THREE-TIER BARRIER."** THE TWO PRIMARY GOALS OF THE OUTERMOST BARRIER WERE TO CONTROL THE SEA AND TO PROJECT AMERICAN MILITARY POWER ASHORE.

THE NAVY'S SEVENTH FLEET FORMED **TASK FORCE 77.** DEPENDING ON MISSION NEEDS, IT WAS COMPOSED OF TWO TO FOUR AIRCRAFT CARRIERS, EACH CARRYING 70 TO 100 AIRCRAFT. IT OPERATED IN THE SOUTH CHINA SEA, OUT OF RANGE OF NORTH VIETNAM'S LITTORAL NAVY, AT A PLACE CODE-NAMED **YANKEE STATION.**

IN THE WORLD WHILE ITS OWN DOMESTIC NEEDS ARE NEGLECTED OR POSTPONED."

IN FEBRUARY 1968, FULBRIGHT CHAIRED **CLOSED-DOOR HEARINGS** TO DETERMINE THE FACTS BEHIND THE TONKIN GULF INCIDENT. FOLLOWING THE HEARINGS, HE DID NOT SUPPORT A CALL FOR A **REPEAL** OF THE RESOLUTION (BECAUSE HE FELT HE COULD NOT MARSHAL ENOUGH VOTES). HE STATED THAT THE RESOLUTION WAS INTRODUCED UNDER "A COMPLETELY FALSE IDEA OF WHAT HAD HAPPENED" AND THAT HE REGRETTED HIS OWN **SUPPORT,** WHICH WAS "BASED UPON INFORMATION WHICH WAS NOT TRUE."

SHORTLY AFTER BECOMING PRESIDENT IN 1969, RICHARD NIXON STATED THAT HE PLANNED TO GRADUALLY WITHDRAW AMERICAN TROOPS FROM VIETNAM. SENATOR FULBRIGHT APPLAUDED THIS MOVE, BUT THEN BECAME DISILLUSIONED WITH NIXON'S **VIETNAMIZATION** POLICY, CALLING IT ANOTHER FORM OF WAGING "A CONTINUING WAR OF STALEMATE AND ATTRITION." IN 1973, FULBRIGHT WAS AN IMPORTANT BACKER OF THE **WAR POWERS ACT,** WHICH LIMITED THE PRESIDENT'S AUTHORITY TO DEPLOY TROOPS OVERSEAS.

FULBRIGHT WAS DEFEATED FOR REELECTION IN 1974. HE DIED IN 1995.

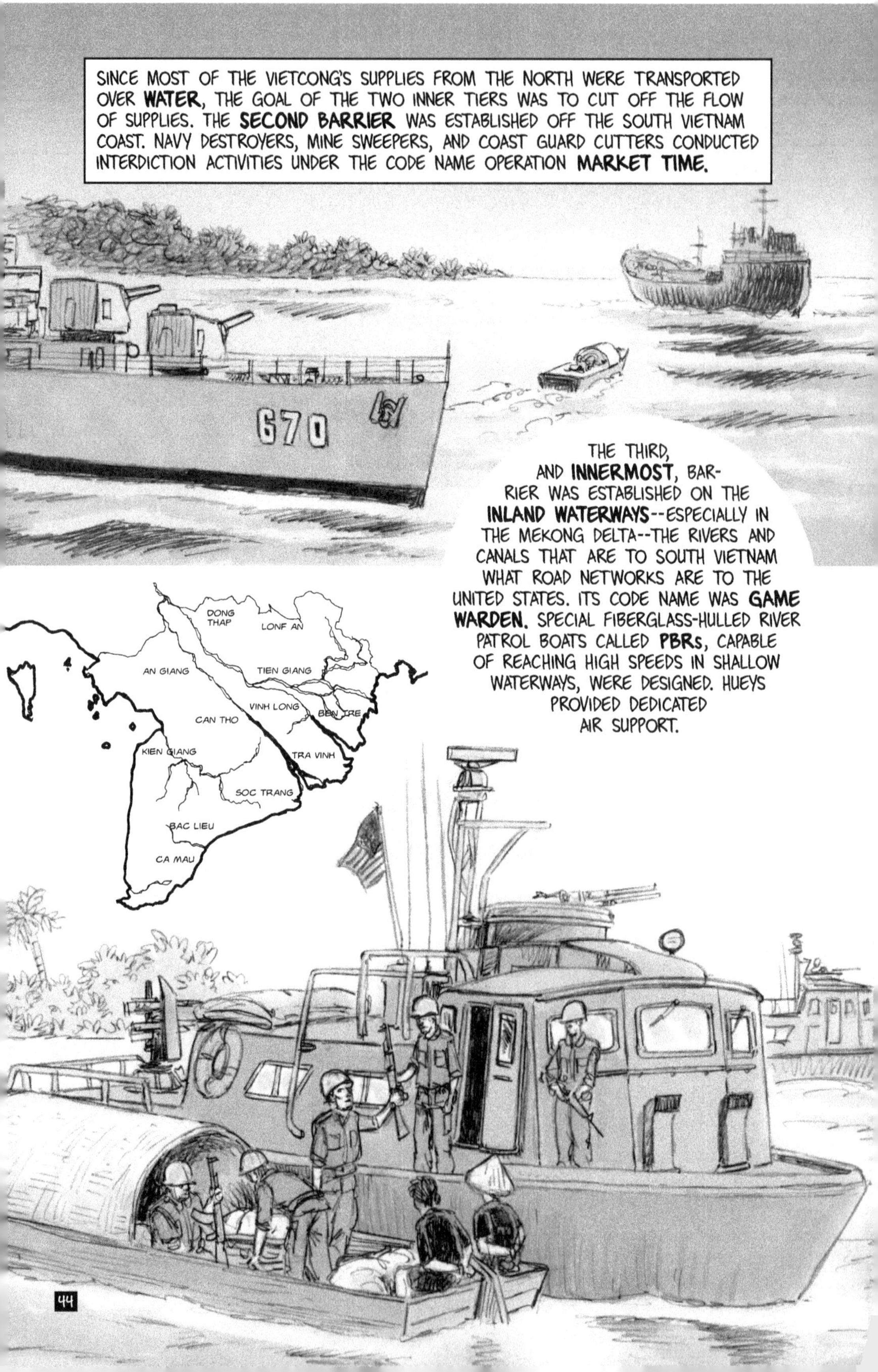
SINCE MOST OF THE VIETCONG'S SUPPLIES FROM THE NORTH WERE TRANSPORTED OVER **WATER**, THE GOAL OF THE TWO INNER TIERS WAS TO CUT OFF THE FLOW OF SUPPLIES. THE **SECOND BARRIER** WAS ESTABLISHED OFF THE SOUTH VIETNAM COAST. NAVY DESTROYERS, MINE SWEEPERS, AND COAST GUARD CUTTERS CONDUCTED INTERDICTION ACTIVITIES UNDER THE CODE NAME OPERATION **MARKET TIME.**
670
THE THIRD, AND **INNERMOST**, BARRIER WAS ESTABLISHED ON THE **INLAND WATERWAYS**--ESPECIALLY IN THE MEKONG DELTA--THE RIVERS AND CANALS THAT ARE TO SOUTH VIETNAM WHAT ROAD NETWORKS ARE TO THE UNITED STATES. ITS CODE NAME WAS **GAME WARDEN.** SPECIAL FIBERGLASS-HULLED RIVER PATROL BOATS CALLED **PBRs**, CAPABLE OF REACHING HIGH SPEEDS IN SHALLOW WATERWAYS, WERE DESIGNED. HUEYS PROVIDED DEDICATED AIR SUPPORT.
DONG THAP
LONF AN
AN GIANG
TIEN GIANG
VINH LONG
BEN TRE
CAN THO
KIEN GIANG
TRA VINH
SOC TRANG
BAC LIEU
CA MAU

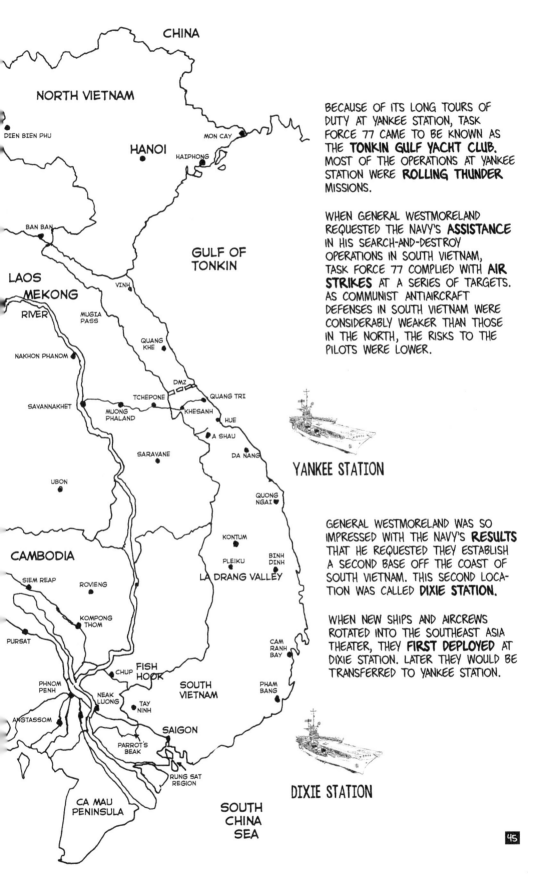

CHINA

NORTH VIETNAM

DIEN BIEN PHU

MON CAY

HANOI

HAIPHONG

BAN BAN

GULF OF
TONKIN

LAOS

MEKONG

VINH

RIVER

MUGIA
PASS

QUANG
KHE

NAKHON PHANOM

DMZ

TCHEPONE

QUANG TRI

SAVANNAKHET

MUONG
PHALAND

KHESANH

HUE

A SHAU

SARAVANE

DA NANG

UBON

QUONG
NGAI

KONTUM

CAMBODIA

PLEIKU

BINH
DINH

SIEM REAP

ROVIENG

LA DRANG VALLEY

KOMPONG
THOM

PURSAT

CAM
RANH
BAY

CHUP

FISH
HOOK

PHNOM
PENH

NEAK
LUONG

TAY
NINH

SOUTH
VIETNAM

PHAM
BANG

ANGTASSOM

SAIGON

PARROT'S
BEAK

RUNG SAT
REGION

CA MAU
PENINSULA

SOUTH
CHINA
SEA

BECAUSE OF ITS LONG TOURS OF
DUTY AT YANKEE STATION, TASK
FORCE 77 CAME TO BE KNOWN AS
THE **TONKIN GULF YACHT CLUB.**
MOST OF THE OPERATIONS AT YANKEE
STATION WERE **ROLLING THUNDER**
MISSIONS.

WHEN GENERAL WESTMORELAND
REQUESTED THE NAVY'S **ASSISTANCE**
IN HIS SEARCH-AND-DESTROY
OPERATIONS IN SOUTH VIETNAM,
TASK FORCE 77 COMPLIED WITH **AIR
STRIKES** AT A SERIES OF TARGETS.
AS COMMUNIST ANTIAIRCRAFT
DEFENSES IN SOUTH VIETNAM WERE
CONSIDERABLY WEAKER THAN THOSE
IN THE NORTH, THE RISKS TO THE
PILOTS WERE LOWER.

YANKEE STATION

GENERAL WESTMORELAND WAS SO
IMPRESSED WITH THE NAVY'S **RESULTS**
THAT HE REQUESTED THEY ESTABLISH
A SECOND BASE OFF THE COAST OF
SOUTH VIETNAM. THIS SECOND LOCA-
TION WAS CALLED **DIXIE STATION.**

WHEN NEW SHIPS AND AIRCREWS
ROTATED INTO THE SOUTHEAST ASIA
THEATER, THEY **FIRST DEPLOYED** AT
DIXIE STATION. LATER THEY WOULD BE
TRANSFERRED TO YANKEE STATION.

DIXIE STATION

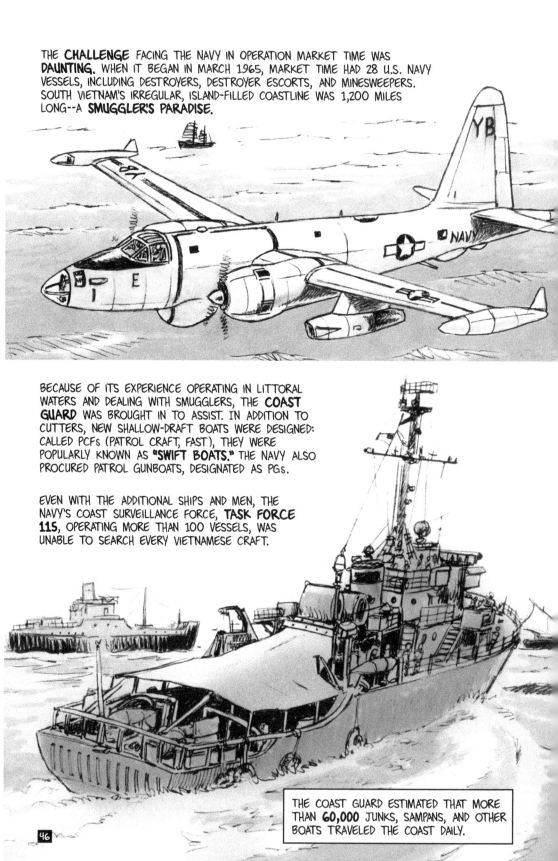

THE **CHALLENGE** FACING THE NAVY IN OPERATION MARKET TIME WAS **DAUNTING.** WHEN IT BEGAN IN MARCH 1965, MARKET TIME HAD 28 U.S. NAVY VESSELS, INCLUDING DESTROYERS, DESTROYER ESCORTS, AND MINESWEEPERS. SOUTH VIETNAM'S IRREGULAR, ISLAND-FILLED COASTLINE WAS 1,200 MILES LONG--A **SMUGGLER'S PARADISE.**

BECAUSE OF ITS EXPERIENCE OPERATING IN LITTORAL WATERS AND DEALING WITH SMUGGLERS, THE **COAST GUARD** WAS BROUGHT IN TO ASSIST. IN ADDITION TO CUTTERS, NEW SHALLOW-DRAFT BOATS WERE DESIGNED: CALLED PCFs (PATROL CRAFT, FAST), THEY WERE POPULARLY KNOWN AS **"SWIFT BOATS."** THE NAVY ALSO PROCURED PATROL GUNBOATS, DESIGNATED AS PGs.

EVEN WITH THE ADDITIONAL SHIPS AND MEN, THE NAVY'S COAST SURVEILLANCE FORCE, **TASK FORCE 115**, OPERATING MORE THAN 100 VESSELS, WAS UNABLE TO SEARCH EVERY VIETNAMESE CRAFT.

THE COAST GUARD ESTIMATED THAT MORE THAN **60,000** JUNKS, SAMPANS, AND OTHER BOATS TRAVELED THE COAST DAILY.

DRAWING ON ITS VAST **EXPERIENCE** WITH SMUGGLERS, THE COAST GUARD ESTABLISHED A **PRIORITIZED LIST** FOR IDENTIFYING AND BOARDING VESSELS.

1) Vessels transiting the area;

2) Junks fishing or operating in restricted areas;

3) Fishing boats anchored and not working nets;

4) Fishing boats working nets.

THAT **JUNK** SEEMS MORE INTERESTED IN **TRAVELING** THAN FISHING. HELMSMAN, **FULL SPEED.** LET'S SEE IF IT'S HIDING SOMETHING.

AYE, SIR.

MANY TIMES THE MEN FOUND **NOTHING.**
A CIA WEEKLY REPORT FOR APRIL 27,
1966, NOTED THAT MARKET TIME FORCES
SEARCHED 4,686 JUNKS AND 18,446
PEOPLE. THE FORCES **DETAINED** 18 OF
THE JUNKS AND 110 PEOPLE.

TO COUNTER **ILL WILL** AMONG FISHERMEN
AND THEIR FAMILIES, AMERICAN SAILORS
PRESENTED SMALL GIFTS OF FOOD OR
OTHER GOODS, OR GAVE **BASIC MEDI-
CAL TREATMENT.** SOMETIMES A MAR-
KET TIME BOAT WOULD BE SURROUNDED
BY VIETNAMESE VESSELS SEEKING **HELP**
FOR ILLS RANGING FROM DENTAL WORK
TO A BROKEN LIMB IN NEED OF SETTING.

SMUGGLERS USED MANY **TACTICS.**
ONE WAS TO SUSPEND **CARGO**
FROM THE BOTTOM OF A HULL.
PATROLS DEVISED A DETECTION
METHOD USING A **DRAGLINE** PULLED
DOWN THE LENGTH OF THE HULL.

THE **RIVERINE FORCE** FOR OPERATION GAME WARDEN, ALSO KNOWN AS THE "BROWN WATER NAVY" BECAUSE OF THE WATER-BORN SILT, FACED MANY OF THE SAME **CHALLENGES** AS THE MARKET TIME SAILORS.

THERE WAS ONE BIG **EXCEPTION**: THEY PATROLLED SOUTH VIETNAM'S NARROWER AND MORE DANGEROUS RIVERS AND CANALS. THEIR MAIN PATROL REGION WAS THE FERTILE **MEKONG DELTA** IN SOUTHERN SOUTH VIETNAM.

THE REGION, AN ALLUVIAL PLAIN THAT CONTAINS ABOUT ONE-FOURTH OF THE TOTAL LAND AREA OF SOUTH VIETNAM, IS ONE OF THE WORLD'S GREAT **RICE-GROWING REGIONS.** VC ACTIVITY THERE WAS INTENSE. AS ONE AMERICAN EMBASSY OFFICIAL STATED, "THAT'S WHERE THE VIETCONG HAVE THEIR HEART, THEIR GREATEST STRENGTH, CONTROL, AND INFLUENCE."

BREAKING THE COMMUNIST **HOLD** IN THE DELTA WOULD NOT BE EASY.

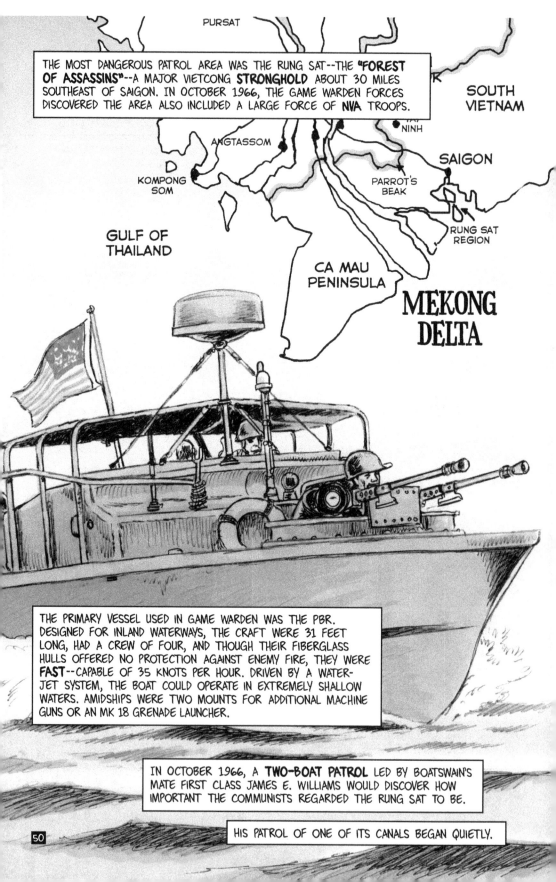

THE MOST DANGEROUS PATROL AREA WAS THE RUNG SAT--THE **"FOREST OF ASSASSINS"**--A MAJOR VIETCONG **STRONGHOLD** ABOUT 30 MILES SOUTHEAST OF SAIGON. IN OCTOBER 1966, THE GAME WARDEN FORCES DISCOVERED THE AREA ALSO INCLUDED A LARGE FORCE OF **NVA** TROOPS.

PURSAT

SOUTH VIETNAM

TAY NINH

ANGTASSOM

SAIGON

KOMPONG SOM

PARROT'S BEAK

GULF OF THAILAND

RUNG SAT REGION

CA MAU PENINSULA

MEKONG DELTA

THE PRIMARY VESSEL USED IN GAME WARDEN WAS THE PBR. DESIGNED FOR INLAND WATERWAYS, THE CRAFT WERE 31 FEET LONG, HAD A CREW OF FOUR, AND THOUGH THEIR FIBERGLASS HULLS OFFERED NO PROTECTION AGAINST ENEMY FIRE, THEY WERE **FAST**--CAPABLE OF 35 KNOTS PER HOUR. DRIVEN BY A WATER-JET SYSTEM, THE BOAT COULD OPERATE IN EXTREMELY SHALLOW WATERS. AMIDSHIPS WERE TWO MOUNTS FOR ADDITIONAL MACHINE GUNS OR AN MK 18 GRENADE LAUNCHER.

IN OCTOBER 1966, A **TWO-BOAT PATROL** LED BY BOATSWAIN'S MATE FIRST CLASS JAMES E. WILLIAMS WOULD DISCOVER HOW IMPORTANT THE COMMUNISTS REGARDED THE RUNG SAT TO BE.

HIS PATROL OF ONE OF ITS CANALS BEGAN QUIETLY.

THEN, IN THE **EARLY EVENING**, THE PBRs ROUNDED A BEND...AND ENCOUNTERED TWO TROOP-FILLED **SAMPANS**. AT FIRST, EVERYONE THOUGHT THEY WERE VIETCONG. BUT--

THOSE AIN'T VC! THEY'RE GODDAMNED **NORTH VIETNAMESE REGULARS!**

WILLIAMS, THE OVERALL COMMANDER, ORDERED HIS BOATS TO **ATTACK**. ONE SAMPAN WAS BEACHED AND **DESTROYED**. THE SECOND SAMPAN TRIED TO ESCAPE DOWN A **CHANNEL** TOO NARROW FOR THE NAVY BOATS TO FOLLOW.

BUT WILLIAMS HAD PATROLLED THE REGION SO MANY TIMES THAT HE KNEW THE CHANNEL'S **EXIT**. IF THEY REACHED THAT POINT QUICKLY ENOUGH, THEY COULD **AMBUSH** THE ENEMY.

BUT WHEN THEY ROUNDED A **BEND** JUST BEFORE THE EXIT POINT, THE SAILORS ON THE TWO PATROL BOATS GOT THE **SURPRISE** OF THEIR LIVES.

51

THEY HAD STUMBLED ONTO THE 261ST AND 262ND NVA **REGIMENTS**. BEFORE THEM WERE AT LEAST 40 SAMPANS FILLED WITH ABOUT **800 ENEMY TROOPS!** MORE TROOPS WERE ON BOTH OF THE CANAL'S BANKS. THE SMART--CERTAINLY THE **SAFE**--THING WOULD HAVE BEEN TO TURN AROUND IMMEDIATELY AND RADIO AN **AIR STRIKE**.

BUT SURPRISE WAS ON WILLIAMS'S SIDE. HE GUNNED HIS BOAT TO **FULL POWER** AND ORDERED HIS TWO-BOAT FORCE TO **ATTACK**.

THEIR ONLY CHANCE TO **DISRUPT** THE ENEMY WAS TO RACE THROUGH THE **MIDDLE** OF THE FORCE.

TO STOP WAS TO **DIE**.

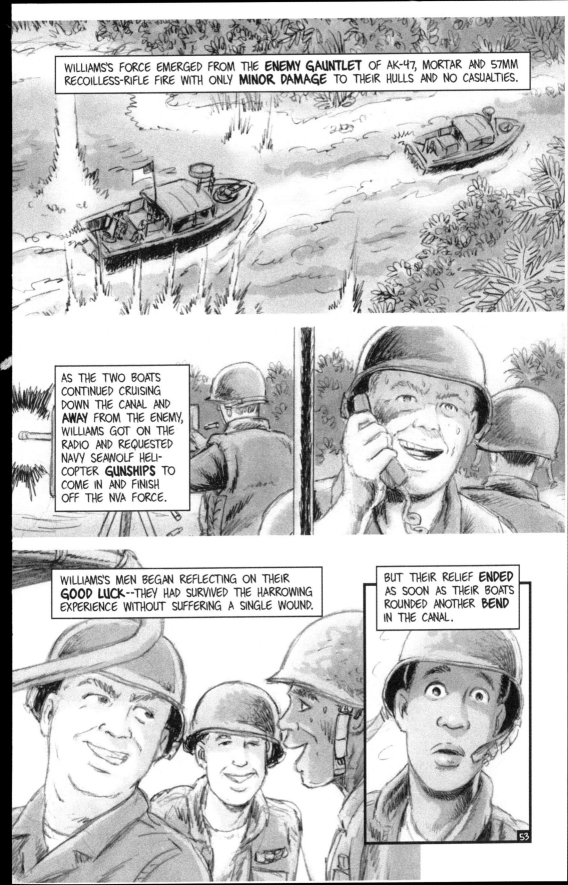

WILLIAMS'S FORCE EMERGED FROM THE **ENEMY GAUNTLET** OF AK-47, MORTAR AND 57MM RECOILLESS-RIFLE FIRE WITH ONLY **MINOR DAMAGE** TO THEIR HULLS AND NO CASUALTIES.

AS THE TWO BOATS CONTINUED CRUISING DOWN THE CANAL AND **AWAY** FROM THE ENEMY, WILLIAMS GOT ON THE RADIO AND REQUESTED NAVY SEAWOLF HELICOPTER **GUNSHIPS** TO COME IN AND FINISH OFF THE NVA FORCE.

WILLIAMS'S MEN BEGAN REFLECTING ON THEIR **GOOD LUCK**--THEY HAD SURVIVED THE HARROWING EXPERIENCE WITHOUT SUFFERING A SINGLE WOUND.

BUT THEIR RELIEF **ENDED** AS SOON AS THEIR BOATS ROUNDED ANOTHER **BEND** IN THE CANAL.

53

WILLIAMS'S MEN FOUND THEMSELVES FACING A SECOND, **LARGER** ENEMY CONVOY. AMAZINGLY, THE ENEMY HAD NOT HEARD THE SOUNDS OF THE EARLIER ENGAGEMENT. **SURPRISE** WAS STILL ON THE SIDE OF THE PBR PATROL.

ONCE AGAIN, WILLIAMS MADE A **QUICK DECISION.** BEFORE THE NORTH VIETNAMESE HAD TIME TO REACT, HE ORDERED A **CHARGE** INTO THEIR MIDST.

ONCE AGAIN, THE TWO PBRs WREAKED **HAVOC** WITH THEIR .50 CALIBER AND M60 (7.62MM) MACHINE GUNS AND LEFT **CHAOS** IN THEIR WAKE.

AND ONCE AGAIN, **AUDACITY** TRUMPED SUPERIOR FORCE. THE AMERICANS MANAGED TO RUN THIS SECOND GAUNTLET SAFELY.

BY THIS TIME, NAVY SEAWOLF HELICOPTERS HAD ARRIVED AND WERE SHOOTING ROCKETS AND FIRING MACHINE GUNS AT THE REELING ENEMY BELOW.

ONE OF THE PILOTS CONTACTED WILLIAMS AND ASKED HIS **INTENTIONS.**

I'M GOIN' BACK THROUGH.

THE BATTLE CONTINUED INTO THE **EVENING**, WITH WILLIAMS AND HIS MEN SEARCHING THE CANAL BANKS AFTER ALL THE **TARGETS** IN THE **WATER** WERE GONE. THREE HOURS AFTER THE FIRST SHOTS WERE FIRED, WILLIAMS ORDERED HIS TWO BOATS TO RETURN TO BASE.

INCREDIBLY, HE AND HIS MEN SUFFERED ONLY TWO SLIGHT WOUNDS. SOME 65 ENEMY SHIPS HAD BEEN **DESTROYED**, AND MORE THAN A THOUSAND **CASUALTIES** INFLICTED.

FOR HIS HEROISM, WILLIAMS RECEIVED THE **MEDAL OF HONOR** FROM PRESIDENT JOHNSON ON MAY 13, 1968.

AIR OPERATIONS DRAMATICALLY INCREASED IN 1966. IN JANUARY, THE ROLLING THUNDER CAMPAIGN RESUMED AFTER A THREE-WEEK SUSPENSION.

THE COMMUNISTS WERE INCREASING THEIR EFFORT AS WELL. MORE MEN AND SUPPLIES WERE BEING SENT SOUTH DOWN THE HO CHI MINH TRAIL.

THE FIRST ATTACKS WERE LAUNCHED ON APRIL 3, 1966, BY NAVY AIRCRAFT OPERATING FROM CARRIERS BASED AT YANKEE STATION.

A SECOND AIR CAMPAIGN, DEVELOPED TO COMPLEMENT ROLLING THUNDER, WAS CODE-NAMED OPERATION STEEL TIGER. ITS PURPOSE WAS TO INTERDICT THE FLOW OF MEN AND SUPPLIES TRAVELING VIA THE HO CHI MINH TRAIL IN LAOS TO COMMUNIST BASES IN SOUTH VIETNAM.

THE MOST EFFECTIVE AIRCRAFT IN STEEL TIGER WERE GUN-SHIPS LIKE THE AC-130S--CALLED SPECTRE AND SPOOKY. ABLE TO FLY OVER A TARGET AREA FOR EXTENDED PERIODS, THE PLANES CARRIED 105MM, 40MM, AND 25MM CANNONS THAT COULD BE FIRED WITH GREAT ACCURACY.

STEEL TIGER MISSIONS STRUCK AT TARGETS WITHIN **LAOS**, A NEUTRAL COUNTRY, AND THE JOHNSON ADMINISTRATION FEARED A DIPLOMATIC **BACKLASH**, OR WORSE. THE SOVIET UNION AND COMMUNIST CHINA WERE ALREADY SUPPLYING NORTH VIETNAM WITH WEAPONS AND ADVISORS. JOHNSON DID NOT WANT TO DO ANYTHING THAT WOULD CAUSE THEM TO SEND **COMBAT TROOPS.**

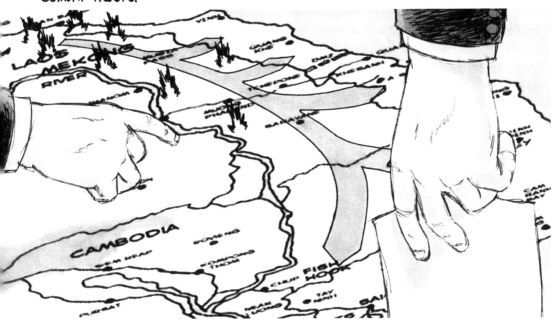

NORTH VIETNAM WAS VIOLATING THE **NEUTRALITY** OF BOTH LAOS AND CAMBODIA BY RUNNING THE HO CHI MINH TRAIL THROUGH THEIR TERRITORY.

THE ADMINISTRATION'S **RESTRICTIONS** IN FLIGHT PATHS, TARGETS, AND RULES OF ENGAGEMENT DENIED MACV PLANNERS THE ABILITY TO ADAPT TO CHANGING TACTICAL SITUATIONS. THOUGH STEEL TIGER WOULD CONTINUE UNTIL DECEMBER 1968, LATER **ANALYSIS** REVEALED IT DID NOT SERIOUSLY **DISRUPT** THE FLOW OF SUPPLIES DOWN THE HO CHI MINH TRAIL.

THE LARGEST WARPLANE IN THE U.S. ARSENAL WAS THE NUCLEAR-BOMB-CARRYING **B-52 STRATOFORTRESS.** IN 1964 THE BOMBERS WERE MODIFIED TO CARRY **CONVENTIONAL BOMBS,** WITH LOADS RANGING FROM 18,000 POUNDS TO 54,000 POUNDS. B-52s WERE ASSIGNED MISSIONS THAT CALLED FOR **AREA BOMBING** OF SUSPECTED ENEMY TROOP CONCENTRATIONS.

ALL B-52 MISSIONS WERE CODE-NAMED **ARC LIGHT** AND WERE COMPOSED OF THREE-PLANE GROUPINGS CALLED CELLS. ORIGINALLY LIMITED TO OPERATIONS OVER SOUTH VIETNAM, IN APRIL 1966, AS PART OF **STEEL TIGER,** ARC LIGHT MISSIONS WERE EXPANDED TO INCLUDE THE HO CHI MINH TRAIL IN NORTHERN LAOS. TAKING OFF FROM BASES IN OKINAWA, GUAM, OR THAILAND, THE B-52s BOMBED TARGETS FROM AN ALTITUDE OF **30,000 FEET,** UNSEEN AND UNHEARD.

THE COMMUNISTS' FIRST **INKLING** THAT THEY WERE UNDER AN ARC LIGHT **ATTACK** WAS WHEN THE BOMBS FELL ON THEM. A NEWSPAPER **REPORT** COMPARED AN ARC LIGHT RAID TO A HOUSEWIFE "SWATTING FLIES WITH A SLEDGEHAMMER."

58

LARGE AREAS OF NORTH AND SOUTH VIETNAM, LAOS, AND CAMBODIA ARE COVERED IN THICK **TROPICAL GROWTH** INCLUDING TRIPLE-CANOPY RAIN FOREST, ELEPHANT GRASS TALLER THAN A MAN, AND CLINGING VINES LIKE THE **"WAIT-A-MINUTE"**--SO-CALLED BECAUSE ANYONE CAUGHT IN THEM SHOUTED, "WAIT A MINUTE!" AS HE FOUGHT TO GET FREE.

THIS LUSH PLANT LIFE MADE **AIR** AND **GROUND SEARCHES** FOR COMMUNIST TROOPS, BASES, AND SUPPLY ROUTES **DIFFICULT.** AS THE THICK JUNGLE BORDERED AMERICAN MILITARY BASES, VIETCONG TROOPS COULD SET UP OBSERVATION POSTS OR **AMBUSHES** WITHOUT BEING DETECTED. FINDING A WAY TO DENY THE ENEMY THIS PROTECTION AND TO DESTROY CROPS IN REGIONS IT CONTROLLED BECAME A PRIORITY.

AS EARLY AS 1961, AMERICANS HAD BEEN EXPERIMENTING WITH **DEFOLIANTS.** IN OCTOBER 1964, **OPERATION RANCH HAND**--THE DEFOLIATION AND CROP DESTRUCTION CAMPAIGN-- WAS LAUNCHED. DIFFERENT TYPES OF **HERBICIDES**, NAMED AFTER THE COLOR-CODING ON THEIR BARRELS, WERE USED FOR DIFFERENT DEFOLIANT PURPOSES.

AGENTS PURPLE, PINK, AND BLUE WERE THE **FIRST HERBICIDES** USED. AGENTS PURPLE AND PINK--CONTAINING **DIOXIN**, THE VIRULENT **TOXICITY** OF WHICH WAS NOT THEN KNOWN--WERE SPRAYED ON JUNGLE AREAS. AGENT BLUE, WHICH DID NOT CONTAIN DIOXIN, WAS USED TO DESTROY CROPS.

THE HERBICIDES WERE DISTRIBUTED IN A VARIETY OF WAYS. **SPRAYERS** WERE MOUNTED ON RIVERBOATS, TRUCKS, OR CARRIED BY MEN. BUT THE PREFERRED METHOD WAS TO USE SPECIALLY RIGGED HELICOPTERS AND **AIRPLANES.**

THE HERBICIDE USED MOST EXTENSIVELY IN VIETNAM FOR JUNGLE DEFOLIATION WAS **AGENT ORANGE.** ABOUT 11.2 MILLION GALLONS WERE SPRAYED.

THE ACTIVE CHEMICAL IN AGENT ORANGE WAS **TCDD**--A DIOXIN THAT INDUCES RAPID, UNCONTROLLED GROWTH IN PLANTS, EVENTUALLY KILLING THEM.

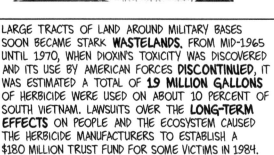

LARGE TRACTS OF LAND AROUND MILITARY BASES SOON BECAME STARK **WASTELANDS.** FROM MID-1965 UNTIL 1970, WHEN DIOXIN'S TOXICITY WAS DISCOVERED AND ITS USE BY AMERICAN FORCES **DISCONTINUED**, IT WAS ESTIMATED A TOTAL OF **19 MILLION GALLONS** OF HERBICIDE WERE USED ON ABOUT 10 PERCENT OF SOUTH VIETNAM. LAWSUITS OVER THE **LONG-TERM EFFECTS** ON PEOPLE AND THE ECOSYSTEM CAUSED THE HERBICIDE MANUFACTURERS TO ESTABLISH A $180 MILLION TRUST FUND FOR SOME VICTIMS IN 1984.

IN 1967, THERE WAS A DRAMATIC **INCREASE** IN BOTH INCOMING TROOPS AND SEARCH-AND-DESTROY OPERATIONS. DESPITE WHITE HOUSE ASSURANCES THAT NO TROOP DEPLOYMENT INCREASES WOULD OCCUR, BY YEAR'S END MORE THAN **485,000 AMERICAN TROOPS** WERE STATIONED IN SOUTH VIETNAM--MORE THAN **DOUBLE** THE NUMBER THERE IN 1965.

THE ADMINISTRATION'S **CREDIBILITY** ABOUT THE WAR'S PROGRESS WAS BEING QUESTIONED. TV NEWS PROGRAMS SHOCKED MANY AMERICANS BECAUSE OF THEIR RAW COMBAT FOOTAGE AND SUGGESTIONS THAT THE FIGHTING WAS BECOMING ENDLESS... AND THE WAR **UNWINNABLE.**

ANTIWAR PROTESTS BECAME MORE NUMEROUS. ON OCTOBER 27, 1967, **PHILIP BERRIGAN,** A CATHOLIC PRIEST, AND THREE OTHERS ENTERED THE SELECTIVE SERVICE OFFICE IN BALTIMORE AND POURED BLOOD ON DRAFT RECORDS. BROUGHT TO TRIAL, HE BECAME THE FIRST ROMAN CATHOLIC PRIEST IN THE UNITED STATES TO BE SENTENCED TO PRISON FOR A **POLITICAL CRIME.**

COMPOUNDING THE GROWING HUMAN COST OF THE WAR WAS ITS **ECONOMIC EXPENSE.** IN THE 1950s, FOREIGN AID TO SOUTH VIETNAM TOTALED ABOUT $250 MILLION. IN 1967, THE JOHNSON ADMINISTRATION REQUESTED FROM CONGRESS A BUDGET OF **$20.3 BILLION** TO FIGHT THE WAR. CONGRESS'S JOINT ECONOMIC COMMITTEE ISSUED A REPORT SAYING THAT THIS SPIKE WAS CREATING **"HAVOC"** IN THE U.S. ECONOMY AND COSTS COULD RUN UP TO $6 BILLION MORE THAN ADMINISTRATION ESTIMATES.

SECRETARY OF DEFENSE MCNAMARA MADE THE CASE BEFORE CONGRESS.

PRESIDENT JOHNSON ASKED GENERAL WEST-MORELAND TO RETURN TO AMERICA AND DO A **WHIRLWIND TOUR** ACROSS THE COUNTRY TO HELP SHORE UP **SUPPORT** FOR THE WAR. ON NOVEMBER 21, 1967, GENERAL WESTMORE-LAND DELIVERED A SPEECH TO THE **NATIONAL PRESS CLUB** IN WASHINGTON, D.C.

I AM **ABSOLUTELY CERTAIN** THAT WHEREAS IN 1965 THE ENEMY WAS WINNING...

...TODAY HE IS CERTAINLY **LOSING.**

WE HAVE REACHED AN IMPORTANT POINT WHEN THE **END** BEGINS TO COME INTO **VIEW.**

HIS **TALK** WAS DUBBED "THE LIGHT AT THE END OF THE TUNNEL" SPEECH. WESTMORELAND RETURNED TO SOUTH VIETNAM, WITH MOST AMERICANS HAVING BEEN **REASSURED** BY HIS WORDS.

PART THREE:
1968: THE YEAR THAT SHOOK THE WORLD

MOST AMERICANS STILL BELIEVED THAT THE UNITED STATES WOULD **WIN** THE WAR IN VIETNAM. THEY JUST DIDN'T UNDERSTAND WHY IT HADN'T HAPPENED YET. MORE AND MORE OF AMERICA'S YOUTH, AND MORE AND MORE TANKS, AIRPLANES, AND OTHER WEAPONS, SUPPLIES, AND EQUIPMENT WERE POURING IN, BUT WITH LITTLE TO SHOW FOR IT. THE **ANTIWAR MOVEMENT,** THOUGH STILL RELATIVELY SMALL, HAD BECOME A STRONG AND VOCAL PRESENCE ON THE POLITICAL LANDSCAPE. AN ANTIWAR "MARCH ON THE PENTAGON" ON OCTOBER 21, 1967, ATTRACTED AN ESTIMATED 50,000 DEMONSTRATORS.

OPINION POLLS TAKEN IN 1967 STARTED SHOWING A DRAMATIC **REDUCTION** IN AMERICAN SUPPORT FOR THE WAR. MORE AND MORE AMERICANS WERE ALSO BECOMING **DISILLUSIONED** WITH THE SUCCESSION OF SOUTH VIETNAM'S GOVERNMENTS. IT SEEMED THAT STARTING WITH NGO DINH DIEM, SOUTH VIETNAM'S FIRST PRESIDENT, THE COUNTRY HAD BEEN WRACKED BY **MISRULE** OF ONE SORT OR ANOTHER. EVEN THE DRAFTING OF A NEW CONSTITUTION IN 1967 FOLLOWED BY A PRESIDENTIAL ELECTION THAT SAME YEAR SEEMED TO RAISE MORE **DOUBTS** IN A GROWING NUMBER OF AMERICAN MINDS. THE TWO MAIN CANDIDATES FOR PRESIDENT, NGUYEN VAN THIEU AND NGUYEN CAO KY, BOTH CAME FROM THE SENIOR RANKS OF THE MILITARY. THOUGH THIEU WON THE ELECTION, KY, NOW THE VICE PRESIDENT, REMAINED A POWERFUL RIVAL.

AGAINST THIS **BACKGROUND** OF A RISING ANTIWAR MOVEMENT...GROWING DISILLUSIONMENT WITH THE WAR AMONG THE AMERICAN POPULACE...A NEW AND STILL-FRAGILE SOUTH VIETNAMESE GOVERNMENT...THE JOHNSON ADMINISTRATION'S PROMISE OF IMMINENT MILITARY VICTORY AGAINST THE COMMUNISTS-- AND A **PRESIDENTIAL ELECTION YEAR**-- AMERICANS WELCOMED 1968.

GENERAL WESTMORELAND WAS CORRECT. **MILI-TARILY,** AMERICA WAS WINNING THE WAR. IN SECRET MEETINGS, THE NORTH VIETNAMESE POLITBURO RECOGNIZED THE TIDE OF WAR WAS TURNING AGAINST THEM. THE **"CROSS-OVER POINT,"** WHERE COMMUNIST TROOP LOSSES EXCEEDED REPLACEMENTS, HAD BEEN REACHED DURING THE FIRST HALF OF 1967.

SECRETARY OF DEFENSE GENERAL VO NGUYEN GIAP'S MAIN POLICY **RIVAL,** GENERAL NGUYEN CHI THANH, DIED IN 1967. OFFICIALLY, THE CAUSE WAS A HEART ATTACK. UNOFFICIALLY, HE WAS KILLED DURING A U.S. **BOMBING RAID.** WITH THANH GONE, GIAP AND HIS ALLIES TOOK THE INITIATIVE AND ADVOCATED THAT THE COMMUNISTS STAGE A SURPRISE, ALL-OUT EFFORT TO SEIZE **VICTORY** IN THE SOUTH.

THE **CAMPAIGN** WOULD CALL FOR A SERIES OF COORDINATED ATTACKS -- TERMED A **GENERAL OFFENSIVE** -- BY THE NVA AND THE VC THROUGHOUT SOUTH VIETNAM. AFTER SOME DELIBERATION, THE POLITBURO AGREED.

TO PREPARE THE GENERAL POPULATION FOR THE **SACRIFICE** TO COME, NORTH VIETNAM'S LEADER, **HO CHI MINH,** SPOKE PUBLICLY TO HIS PEOPLE. SUCH WAS HIS PRESTIGE IN THE COUNTRY THAT HE SUCCEEDED IN RALLYING THEIR **SUPPORT.**

THE POLITBURO BELIEVED THEIR GENERAL OFFENSIVE WOULD DEFEAT THE SOUTH VIETNAMESE ARMY. THIS WOULD INSPIRE WHAT THEY TERMED A **GENERAL UPRISING** BY THE SOUTH VIETNAMESE POPULACE AGAINST ITS GOVERNMENT.

AS THE COMMUNISTS SAW IT, THIS **ONE-TWO PUNCH** OF MILITARY VICTORY AND POPULAR SUPPORT WOULD FORCE THE AMERICANS TO RECOGNIZE THEIR UNTENABLE POSITION, **CAPITULATE**, AND LEAVE SOUTH VIETNAM.

PLANNING FOR THE GENERAL OFFENSIVE BEGAN IN JULY 1967. THE **BUILDUP** OF SUPPLIES IN CACHES THROUGHOUT LAOS, CAMBODIA, AND SOUTH VIETNAM BEGAN SOON AFTER. THE **START DATE** WAS SET FOR THE BEGINNING OF **TET**, THE VIETNAMESE NEW YEAR, ON JANUARY 30, 1968.

JUST BEFORE THE GENERAL OFFENSIVE WAS LAUNCHED, GENERAL GIAP PLANNED A **DECEPTION** TO PULL U.S. TROOPS AWAY FROM HIS **REAL TARGETS.**

THE KEY WAS A **DIVERSIONARY ATTACK** ON THE REMOTE MARINE OUTPOST AT **KHE SANH.** GENERAL GIAP PREDICTED THAT THE AMERICANS WOULD SEE THE **PARALLEL** TO HIS 1954 ATTACK ON THE FRENCH OUTPOST AT **DIEN BIEN PHU.**

THAT BATTLE HAD TURNED INTO A **SIEGE** THAT LASTED FROM MARCH 13 TO MAY 7, 1954. IT WAS THE CLIMACTIC BATTLE BETWEEN THE **VIETMINH,** AS THE COMMUNIST INSURGENCY WAS THEN CALLED, AND FRENCH COLONIAL RULERS IN A WAR OF **LIBERATION** THAT HAD BEGUN IN EARNEST IN 1946. LESS THAN THREE MONTHS AFTER THE FRENCH GARRISON CAPITULATED, THE FRENCH GOVERNMENT SIGNED A **PEACE TREATY** WITH THE VIETMINH ON JULY 20, 1954, ENDING ALMOST 100 YEARS OF COLONIAL RULE.

THE ATTACK ON KHE SANH WAS PART OF GIAP'S **"PERIPHERAL CAMPAIGN"** TARGETING AMERICAN AND SOUTH VIETNAMESE ARMY MILITARY BASES SOUTH OF THE DMZ. ITS PURPOSE, PARTICULARLY AT KHE SANH, WAS TO DRAW AS MANY TROOPS AS POSSIBLE AWAY FROM THE ACTUAL **STRATEGIC OBJECTIVE** OF THE CAMPAIGN--THE AREA IN SOUTHERN SOUTH VIETNAM KNOWN AS **"THE SAIGON CIRCLE."**

THE SAIGON CIRCLE WAS COMPOSED OF THE SOUTH VIETNAMESE CAPITAL CITY OF SAIGON AND THE LARGE MILITARY BASES AT NEARBY LONG BINH AND BIEN HOA. THE COMMUNISTS HAD **EIGHT MAJOR OBJECTIVES** IN THE CIRCLE THAT, ONCE CAPTURED, THEY BELIEVED WOULD **CRIPPLE** THE SOUTH VIETNAMESE GOVERNMENT AND HELP **TRIGGER** A PRO-COMMUNIST UPRISING.

THE **OBJECTIVES** IN SAIGON INCLUDED ALL KEY GOVERNMENT COMMAND, CONTROL, AND COM-MUNICATIONS CENTERS, THE ARTILLERY AND TANK DEPOTS AT GO VAP, THE **NEUTRALIZATION** OF THE MILITARY BASE AND MACV HEADQUARTERS AT NEARBY TAN SON NHUT AIR BASE, AND THE NEWPORT BRIDGE THAT LINKED SAIGON TO LONG BINH AND BIEN HOA.

AT LONG BINH, THE PRIMARY OBJECTIVE WAS THE LARGE U.S. **LOGISTICS DEPOT** AND U.S. II FIELD FORCE HEADQUARTERS. AT BIEN HOA, THE PRIMARY TARGETS WERE THE U.S. AIR BASE AND THE SOUTH VIETNAMESE ARMY III CORPS **HEADQUARTERS.** OTHER COMMUNIST TROOPS WERE MOVED INTO POSITION TO **PREVENT** THE AMERICANS AND SOUTH VIETNAMESE FROM **REINFORCING** UNITS WITHIN THE SAIGON CIRCLE.

IN DECEMBER 1967, AS THE TET NEW YEAR APPROACHED, MACV INTELLIGENCE BEGAN RECEIVING REPORTS SHOWING UNUSUAL ENEMY **COMMUNICATIONS** AND **TROOP MOVEMENT** PATTERNS.

IN RESPONSE, AMERICAN COMMANDERS STEPPED UP THE NUMBER OF **PATROLS,** PARTICULARLY AROUND **KHE SANH.** THIS LARGE AND ISOLATED U.S. MARINE BASE -- SIX MILES FROM THE SOUTH VIETNAM/LAOS BORDER AND 14 MILES SOUTH OF THE DMZ -- WAS LOCATED NEAR ONE OF THE MAJOR COMMUNIST **INFILTRATION ROUTES** ON THE HO CHI MINH TRAIL.

IN PREVIOUS YEARS BOTH SIDES HAD AGREED TO A **TRUCE** FOR TET, THE MOST IMPORTANT HOLIDAY ON THE VIETNAMESE CALENDAR, THOUGH OCCASIONALLY RANDOM AND UNCOORDINATED **FIGHTING** DID CONTINUE. THIS TIME, SOME OF THE SENIOR AMERICAN GENERALS BEGAN TO **SUSPECT** THAT THE COMMUNISTS WERE PLANNING SOMETHING **BIGGER.** THEY JUST DIDN'T KNOW HOW BIG.

THEIR SUSPICIONS WERE CONFIRMED ON JANUARY 20, WHEN A MARINE PLATOON OF ABOUT 20 MEN **STUMBLED ONTO** A BATTALION-SIZED UNIT OF APPROXIMATELY 500 NVA TROOPS NEAR KHE SANH AND CAME **UNDER FIRE.**

WHAT THE MARINES AT KHE SANH COULD NOT KNOW WAS THAT THEIR PATROL HAD **PREMATURELY TRIPPED**, BY 10 DAYS, THE NVA'S GENERAL OFFENSIVE.

THE CHANCE ENCOUNTER CAUSED THE COMMUNISTS TO **MOVE UP** THE DATE OF THEIR **ATTACK** OF KHE SANH TO THE FOLLOWING DAY. ON JANUARY 21, AN INTENSE ROCKET AND ARTILLERY **BARRAGE** HIT THE MARINES' MAIN AMMUNITION DUMP.

KA-BWOOM

THE 6,000 MARINES AT KHE SANH WERE SOON **SURROUNDED** BY MORE THAN 30,000 ENEMY TROOPS--AND WERE DESPERATELY SHORT OF **AMMUNITION.**

THE ONLY WAY TO **SUPPLY** THE MARINES WAS THROUGH THE **AIR.** BUT THE NORTH VIETNAMESE NOOSE OF ARTILLERY AND ANTIAIRCRAFT GUNS AROUND THE BASE WAS TIGHT. A **FLIGHT** OF CARGO PLANES ARRIVING LATER ON JANUARY 21 WAS ABLE TO DELIVER **24 TONS** OF CARGO.

BUT **COLONEL DAVID LOWNDS,** COMMANDER OF THE MARINES AT KHE SANH, ESTIMATED HE NEEDED **160 TONS** OF SUPPLIES **A DAY** TO HOLD OUT.

THE AMERICANS REACTED AS GENERAL GIAP **EXPECTED.** GENERAL WESTMORELAND VOWED THAT KHE SANH WOULD NOT BE ANOTHER **DIEN BIEN PHU.**

WE ARE NOT, REPEAT **NOT,** GOING TO BE DEFEATED AT KHE SANH.

I WILL TOLERATE NO TALKING OR EVEN **THINKING** TO THE CONTRARY.

AS THE **SIEGE** CONTINUED, PRESIDENT JOHNSON BECAME SO CONCERNED HE ORDERED A **MODEL** OF THE BASE BUILT AND HAD HOURLY **UPDATES.**

BUT GIAP HAD **MISCALCULATED** THE EXTENT OF AMERICAN **AIR POWER.** U.S. FIGHTER-BOMBERS FLEW AN AVERAGE OF 300 SORTIES A DAY. THEY WERE JOINED BY B-52 ARC LIGHT STRIKES THAT **BOMBED** NORTH VIETNAMESE ARMY COMMAND CENTERS IN LAOS, AND AT COMMUNIST POSITIONS AS CLOSE AS **1,000 YARDS** OF THE MARINE PERIMETER AT KHE SANH. SUPPLIES INCREASED AFTER THE FIRST DAY OF THE SIEGE AND **MORALE** AMONG THE MARINES REMAINED **HIGH.**

WHEN THE SIEGE WAS FINALLY LIFTED IN EARLY MARCH, THE MARINES HAD SUFFERED ALMOST 1,900 **CASUALTIES,** INCLUDING 205 KILLED IN ACTION. COLONEL LOWNDS WAS CONVINCED THAT THE NORTH VIETNAMESE CASUALTIES DURING THE SIEGE WERE SO HIGH THAT ENTIRE **DIVISIONS,** TOTALING ABOUT 35,000 MEN, WERE EFFECTIVELY **DESTROYED.**

LT. GENERAL FREDERICK WEYAND, COMMANDER OF U.S. II FIELD FORCES BASED IN LONG BINH, WAS ONE OF THE SENIOR COMMANDERS TO RECEIVE THE INTELLIGENCE ASSESSMENTS OF THE UNUSUAL NVA **COMMUNICATIONS ACTIVITY AND TROOP MOVEMENTS** FROM DECEMBER 1967 TO JANUARY 1968.

THIS REPORT SAYS THE VIETCONG HAVE RE-ORGANIZED THEIR COMMAND STRUCTURE. YET "NO EX-PLANATION IS AVAILABLE AS TO THE REASON FOR THIS REORGANIZATION."

THESE REPORTS RAISED WEYAND'S SUSPICIONS. HE QUICKLY WENT TO GENERAL WESTMORELAND.

I DON'T KNOW WHAT THE COMMUNISTS HAVE GOT IN MIND, BUT THERE'S AN ATTACK COMING.

WEYAND REQUESTED A **POSTPONEMENT** OF HIS UPCOMING PREEMPTIVE ATTACKS NEAR THE CAMBODIAN BORDER AND THAT HIS TROOPS BE **REDEPLOYED** CLOSER TO SAIGON. THIS REINFORCED WESTMORELAND'S OWN SUSPICIONS.

I AGREE. THE ATTACKS ARE CANCELED. REDEPLOY THE TROOPS.

AS A RESULT, INSTEAD OF **14 BATTALIONS** AND APPROXIMATELY 12,600 MEN, **27 BATTALIONS** AND APPROXIMATELY 24,300 TROOPS WERE STATIONED IN THE SAIGON CIRCLE IN JANUARY 1968. IT WAS A MOVE THAT WOULD HAVE IMPORTANT **CONSEQUENCES.**

GENERAL GIAP SCHEDULED THE COUNTRYWIDE GENERAL OFFENSIVE TO COMMENCE ON THE **FIRST DAY** OF TET, WHICH, ACCORDING TO THE LUNAR CALENDAR AUTHORIZED BY THE POLIT-BURO, FELL ON **JANUARY 31, 1968.** BUT, SOME FIELD COMMANDERS IN SOUTH VIETNAM MIS-TAKENLY USED **SOUTH VIETNAM'S** LUNAR CALENDAR, WHICH HAD TET BEGINNING A DAY EARLIER. AS A RESULT, COMMUNISTS ATTACKED DA NANG AND ELEVEN OTHER CITIES ON **JANUARY 30.**

IT WAS THE DIFFERENCE OF ONLY **ONE** DAY, BUT IT WAS ENOUGH TO **ALERT** THE AMERICANS AND SOUTH VIETNAMESE.

THE MEDIA IN THE VIETNAM WAR: PART ONE

THE VIETNAM WAR WAS THE MOST REPORTED-ON CONFLICT TO DATE IN THE HISTORY OF WARFARE. IN 1964 THERE WERE ONLY 40 ACCREDITED U.S. AND FOREIGN JOURNALISTS IN SOUTH VIETNAM. BY 1966, THERE WERE 419. EVENTUALLY **500 JOURNALISTS** REPRESENTING MORE THAN 130 NEWS ORGANIZATIONS OPERATED IN THE THEATER. SOME OF THE MOST FAMOUS AND **RESPECTED REPORTERS** IN MODERN JOURNALISM BEGAN OR MADE THEIR **REPUTATIONS** WITH THEIR REPORTAGE FROM VIETNAM, INCLUDING HOMER BIGART AND **DAVID HALBERSTAM** OF *THE NEW YORK TIMES*, PETER ARNETT AND MALCOLM BROWNE OF THE ASSOCIATED PRESS, PETER KALISCHER OF CBS NEWS, **NEIL SHEEHAN** OF UNITED PRESS INTERNATIONAL, PETER BRAESTRUP OF *THE WASHINGTON POST*, AND PHOTOJOURNALIST **HORST FAAS.** A NUMBER OF THEM WOULD WIN **PULITZER PRIZES** EITHER FOR THEIR REPORTING DURING THE WAR OR FOR LATER HISTORIES ABOUT THE WAR.

JOURNALISTS IN SOUTH VIETNAM WORKED UNDER EXTRAORDINARILY DIFFICULT AND **STRESSFUL CONDITIONS**, PARTICULARLY IN THE EARLY 1960S. CELL PHONES, FAXES, INTERNET, NONMILITARY OVERNIGHT AIR COURIER SYSTEMS, EVEN PRIVATE OVERSEAS PHONE LINES, DID NOT YET **EXIST.** THE AMERICAN MILITARY WAS NOT OBLIGATED TO HELP JOURNALISTS FILE THEIR STORIES. OVERSEAS TELEPHONE AND TELEGRAPH CALLS AND

ON THE MORNING OF JANUARY 31, THE **TET OFFENSIVE**, AS IT CAME TO BE KNOWN, BEGAN IN EARNEST WITH SIMULTANEOUS ATTACKS IN AND AROUND ALMOST **40 CITIES** THROUGHOUT SOUTH VIETNAM. THOUGH ALERTED, THE EXTENT OF THE OFFENSIVE TOOK MACV BY **SURPRISE.** THE COMMUNISTS WERE THOUGHT NOT TO HAVE THE CAPABILITY NEEDED TO COORDINATE SUCH A **MASSIVE EFFORT.**

MESSAGES WERE EXPENSIVE AND HAD TO GO THROUGH MESSAGE CENTERS AT THE LOCAL POST OFFICE THAT, BECAUSE THEY WERE UNDER **GOVERNMENT CONTROL,** WERE SUBJECT TO CENSORSHIP. IN ADDITION, LOCAL OFFICIALS WERE NOTORIOUSLY **CORRUPT.** NEIL SHEEHAN ONCE HAD TO BRIBE A POST OFFICE SUPERVISOR WITH A BRAND NEW TYPEWRITER IN ORDER TO MAKE SURE PHONE CALLS TO HIS EDITOR WENT THROUGH.

THE AMERICAN JOURNALISTS WERE AS **PATRIOTIC** AS THE MEN IN UNIFORM FIGHTING THE WAR. BUT NEWS REPORTING IS A **BUSINESS,** AND A COMPETITIVE ONE--BEATING THE COMPETITION TO A STORY IS ALWAYS ON REPORTERS' MINDS. AMERICAN GOVERNMENT POLICY PROMOTED DEMOCRATIC SOUTH VIETNAM AS A SHINING **BULWARK** AGAINST COMMUNISM. REPORTERS SAW THE INEPTNESS AND **CORRUPTION** OF THE SOUTH VIETNAMESE GOVERNMENT AND THE RELUCTANCE OF ITS MILITARY TO FIGHT--AND THEY WROTE ABOUT IT. THEIR REPORTS, WHICH CONSISTENTLY CONFLICTED WITH THE OPTIMISTIC ONES FROM THE MILITARY COMMANDERS, QUICKLY PUT THEM AT **ODDS** WITH THE WHITE HOUSE.

FOR THE MOST PART, REPORTERS IN SOUTH VIETNAM DELIVERED **ACCURATE NEWS,** AND MANY MILITARY COMMANDERS LATER COMMENTED THAT THE JOURNALISTS WHO FILED THE **BEST REPORTS** WERE THOSE WHO ACCOMPANIED THE TROOPS INTO THE **FIELD.**

SOON, **REPORTS** OF THE COMMUNIST ATTACK BEGAN TO PILE UP IN MACV HEADQUARTERS. **ORDERS** WERE IMMEDIATELY ISSUED. GENERAL WEYAND WAS ORDERED TO SEND TROOPS INTO SAIGON TO REINFORCE UNITS ALREADY THERE AND TO HELP **DEFEND** THE AMERICAN EMBASSY AND OTHER GOVERNMENT LOCATIONS.

APPROXIMATELY 4,000 COMMUNIST TROOPS WERE ASSIGNED TO THE **ASSAULT** ON SAIGON. ONE VIETCONG SAPPER BATTALION OF 250 COMBAT ENGINEERS WAS CHARGED WITH **SIX OBJEC-TIVES,** INCLUDING THE CONTROL OF THE SOUTH VIETNAMESE PRESIDENTIAL PALACE...

...AND THE **AMERICAN EMBASSY.** A 19-MAN VIETCONG PLATOON ATTACKED THE AMERICAN EMBASSY JUST BEFORE 3:00 A.M. THEY MANAGED TO **BREACH** THE WALL WITH SATCHEL CHARGES AND ENTER THE **COURTYARD.**

THAT WAS AS FAR AS THEY GOT. THE VIETCONG WERE **TRAPPED.** BY 9:15 A.M. THE FIGHT FOR THE EMBASSY WAS OVER AND THE COMPOUND DECLARED **SECURE** BY THE AMERICAN COMMANDER. THE VIETCONG HAD BEEN SUCCESSFULLY **REPULSED** FROM THE PRESIDENTIAL PALACE AS WELL.

ANOTHER VIETCONG PLATOON SEIZED THE **NATIONAL RADIO STATION** NORTH OF SAIGON. THEY HAD RECORDED **TAPES** TO ANNOUNCE THE OFFENSIVE TO THE SOUTH VIETNAMESE AND URGE THEM TO JOIN IN A **GENERAL UPRISING.**

BUT THE MESSAGE **NEVER** WENT OUT.

TECHNICIANS AT THE STATION'S TRANSMITTER, LOCATED ELSEWHERE, SEVERED THE **POWER CABLE.**

ON THE AIR

IN OTHER LOCATIONS, THE VC **SUCCEEDED** IN MAKING THEIR **BROADCASTS.** BUT INSTEAD OF RISING UP IN **REVOLT** AGAINST THEIR GOVERNMENT, THE SOUTH VIETNAMESE **UNITED** BEHIND IT. THE GENERAL UPRISING PROVED A COLOSSAL AND EMBARRASSING **FAILURE** FOR THE COMMUNISTS.

75

ON THE **FIRST DAY**, FIVE OF SIX AUTONOMOUS CITIES, 36 OF 44 PROVINCIAL CAPITALS, AND 64 OF 245 DISTRICT CAPITALS WERE **ATTACKED**.

THE LARGEST AND BLOODIEST **BATTLE** DURING THE OFFENSIVE WAS AT **HUE**, THE CITY THAT HAD BEEN THE ANCIENT IMPERIAL CAPITAL OF VIETNAM AND WAS NOW THE CULTURAL AND INTELLECTUAL **CENTER** OF THE COUNTRY.

A COMBINED FORCE TOTALING NINE VC AND NVA BATTALIONS--MORE THAN **4,500 TROOPS**--PARTICIPATED IN THE INITIAL **ATTACK**. THEY SEIZED THE HISTORIC IMPERIAL **CITADEL** AND ITS PALACE OF SUPREME PEACE. AS THE FIGHTING CONTINUED, ANOTHER 2,500 TROOPS FROM FIVE MORE NVA BATTALIONS JOINED IN THE FIGHT.

MACV HAD UNDERESTIMATED THE SIZE AND NATURE OF THE **THREAT**. THE 1ST MARINE DIVISION BASED IN NEARBY PHU BAI INITIALLY RESPONDED WITH **PIECEMEAL DEPLOYMENTS** OF TROOPS. SOON ARMY, MARINE, AND SOUTH VIETNAMESE ARMY (ARVN) **REINFORCEMENTS** RUSHED IN. IT WOULD TAKE ALMOST A **MONTH** OF HARD FIGHTING BEFORE ALLIED FORCES RECAPTURED THE CITADEL AND CLEARED THE COMMUNISTS OUT OF HUE.

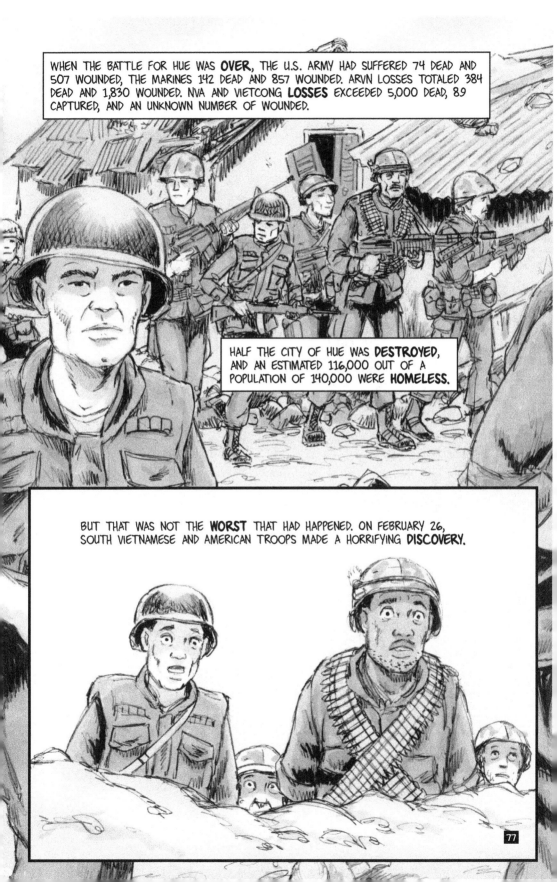

WHEN THE BATTLE FOR HUE WAS **OVER**, THE U.S. ARMY HAD SUFFERED 74 DEAD AND 507 WOUNDED, THE MARINES 142 DEAD AND 857 WOUNDED. ARVN LOSSES TOTALED 384 DEAD AND 1,830 WOUNDED. NVA AND VIETCONG **LOSSES** EXCEEDED 5,000 DEAD, 89 CAPTURED, AND AN UNKNOWN NUMBER OF WOUNDED.

HALF THE CITY OF HUE WAS **DESTROYED**, AND AN ESTIMATED 116,000 OUT OF A POPULATION OF 140,000 WERE **HOMELESS**.

BUT THAT WAS NOT THE **WORST** THAT HAD HAPPENED. ON FEBRUARY 26, SOUTH VIETNAMESE AND AMERICAN TROOPS MADE A HORRIFYING **DISCOVERY**.

DURING THEIR ONE-MONTH **OCCUPATION** OF HUE, THE VIETCONG CONDUCTED THOROUGH NEIGHBORHOOD **SWEEPS.** THEY WERE LOOKING FOR FOREIGNERS, INTELLECTUALS, RELIGIOUS AND POLITICAL LEADERS, AND OTHER "CRUEL TYRANTS AND REACTIONARY ELEMENTS."

THESE PEOPLE WERE TAKEN AWAY AND **EXECUTED,** SOME AFTER THEY HAD BEEN **TORTURED.** A TOTAL OF 2,810 BODIES BURIED IN MASS GRAVES WERE FOUND, WITH THE TOTAL CIVILIAN **DEATH COUNT** ESTIMATED AS HIGH AS 5,700.

BEFORE THE BATTLE, THE LOCAL POPULATION WAS FOR THE MOST PART **NEUTRAL,** BUT THE ATROCITIES HARDENED THEM **AGAINST** THE COMMUNISTS.

THOUGH THE MAIN FIGHTING DURING THE TET OFFENSIVE OCCURRED ON LAND, THERE WAS ONE IMPORTANT **NAVAL ACTION.** MARKET TIME PATROLS HAD MADE THE COASTAL SUPPLY ROUTE HAZARDOUS, SO THE SUPPLY REQUIREMENTS OF THE SOUTHERNMOST VC FORCES REQUIRED AN **ALL-OUT EFFORT** FROM THE NORTH VIETNAMESE NAVY. FOUR TRAWLERS WERE DISPATCHED WITH SUPPLIES FOR THE OFFENSIVE.

AT 5:00 P.M. ON FEBRUARY 29 (1968 BEING A LEAP YEAR), COAST GUARD CUTTER *ANDROSCOGGIN*, ON STATION OFF THE COAST OF QUANG NGAI PROVINCE APPROXIMATELY 100 MILES SOUTH OF DA NANG, RECEIVED AN **ALERT** FROM A MARKET TIME PATROL AIRCRAFT THAT HAD SIGHTED A SUSPICIOUS-LOOKING **TRAWLER.**

THE *ANDROSCOGGIN'S* RADAR PICKED UP THE **TRAWLER** IN INTERNATIONAL WATERS AT ALMOST 9:00 P.M. AND, WHILE STAYING OUTSIDE VISUAL CONTACT, BEGAN **SHADOWING** IT.

WHEN THE TRAWLER CROSSED THE **12-MILE LIMIT** AND ENTERED SOUTH VIETNAMESE TERRITORIAL WATERS, THE *ANDROSCOGGIN* CLOSED IN. JUST AFTER 1:00 A.M. ON MARCH 1, SHE ISSUED A **CHALLENGE**. IT WAS IGNORED.

THE TRAWLER TRIED TO **ESCAPE**, BUT REINFORCEMENTS, INCLUDING OTHER CUTTERS AND PCF BOATS, AS WELL AS HELICOPTER **GUNSHIPS** AND AN AIR FORCE PLANE DROPPING **FLARES**, QUICKLY ARRIVED.

THE TRAWLER RAN **AGROUND**, WHERE HER CAPTAIN SET OFF **EXPLOSIVE CHARGES** TO PREVENT THE CARGO FROM BEING CAPTURED.

KA-ROOM

AT THE SAME TIME, 50 MILES **SOUTH**, A COMBINED FORCE OF FOUR COAST GUARD CUTTERS AND SEVERAL NAVY PCF PATROL BOATS ATTACKED AND DESTROYED A **SECOND TRAWLER**.

MEANWHILE, 100 MILES **SOUTH** OF THE SECOND ACTION, A **THIRD TRAWLER** WAS INTERCEPTED, BEACHED, AND **DESTROYED.**

A **FOURTH TRAWLER**, STEAMING FROM CAMBODIA, WAS **DISCOVERED** AS IT WAS ABOUT TO ENTER SOUTH VIETNAMESE WATERS FROM THE WEST. IT **REVERSED COURSE** BEFORE IT COULD BE INTERCEPTED AND ATTACKED.

IT WAS ONLY WELL AFTER MARKET TIME HAD COME TO AN END THAT U.S. NAVY SENIOR COMMANDERS REALIZED THAT THEIR FORCES HAD ENGAGED IN THE **LARGEST NAVAL ACTION** OF THE VIETNAM WAR--ONE THAT HAD COVERED THE **ENTIRE LENGTH** OF THE COAST.

BY **MARCH 20, 1968**, THE TET OFFENSIVE WAS OVER. THE COMMUNISTS HAD SUFFERED **DEFEATS** THROUGHOUT SOUTH VIETNAM.

A COPY OF A **FIVE-PAGE DOCUMENT**, WRITTEN ON FEBRUARY 1 BY MEMBERS OF NORTH VIETNAM'S RULING **POLITBURO** BASED IN SOUTH VIETNAM, AND CAPTURED ON FEBRUARY 9, REVEALED THE **STUNNING FACT** THAT THE COMMUNISTS REALIZED THAT THE OFFENSIVE HAD **FAILED** AS EARLY AS TWO DAYS AFTER IT BEGAN.

THEY WROTE, **IN PART**, "WE FAILED TO SEIZE A NUMBER OF PRIMARY OBJECTIVES AND TO DESTROY MOBILE AND DEFENSIVE UNITS OF THE ENEMY."

"IN THE POLITICAL FIELD, WE FAILED TO MOTIVATE THE PEOPLE TO STAGE UPRISINGS." IT **CONCLUDED** WITH THE STATEMENT "WE CANNOT YET, THEREFORE, ACHIEVE TOTAL VICTORY IN A SHORT PERIOD." BUT, ONCE HAVING **LAUNCHED** THE ATTACK, THEY WERE CAUGHT IN A **CYCLE OF BATTLE** FROM WHICH IT WAS IMPOSSIBLE TO **DISENGAGE** QUICKLY.

THE OFFENSIVE WAS A **MILITARY DISASTER** FOR THE COMMUNISTS. THEY FAILED TO ACHIEVE ANY OF THEIR **TACTICAL OBJECTIVES** IN SOUTH VIETNAM. MORE THAN 58,000 VC AND NVA TROOPS WERE **KILLED.** APPROXIMATELY 4,300 AMERICAN AND SOUTH VIETNAMESE TROOPS WERE KILLED AND 16,000 WERE WOUNDED.

THE VIETCONG WAS VIRTUALLY **WIPED OUT.** NEVER AGAIN WOULD IT BE A **SIGNIFICANT** FORCE IN THE WAR.

YET, FROM THE ASHES OF THEIR **TACTICAL DEFEAT,** THE COMMUNISTS ACHIEVED A DECISIVE **STRATEGIC VICTORY--** ONE WHOSE SCOPE THEY HAD NO WAY OF FORESEEING.

END THE WAR NOW!

EN THE O NO

HELL NO! WE WON GO!

AMERICA OUT OF SOUTH VIETNAM!

AMERICA OUT OF SOUTH VIETNAM!

HELL NO! WE WON'T GO!

NEWS REPORTS OF THE TET OFFENSIVE HIT THE AMERICAN PUBLIC LIKE A **THUNDERBOLT.**

EVERYONE--FROM SAVVY POLITICAL INSIDERS TO RESIDENTS OF MAIN STREET AMERICA--WAS TAKEN **ABACK.**

THE COMMON QUESTION ASKED WAS, IF WE WERE WINNING, **HOW** COULD THE ENEMY LAUNCH SUCH AN ATTACK?

STUDENT PROTESTS

POLITICAL ACTIVISM AMONG COLLEGE STUDENTS IN THE EARLY 1960S WAS INITIALLY FOCUSED ON CIVIL RIGHTS ISSUES. MOST GROUPS WERE LOCAL, REGIONALLY FOCUSED, AND NOT FORMALLY LINKED TO OTHER CAMPUSES. AN EXCEPTION WAS THE **STUDENTS FOR A DEMOCRATIC SOCIETY,** OR SDS. THOUGH A NATIONAL ORGANIZATION WITH A HEADQUARTERS, MOST AUTHORITY WAS DECENTRALIZED AND HELD BY THE LOCAL COLLEGE CHAPTERS.

WHEN IN 1965 PRESIDENT JOHNSON AUTHORIZED MILITARY GROUND OPERATIONS AND AN INCREASE IN TROOP STRENGTH IN VIETNAM, THE SDS NATIONAL ORGANIZATION FOCUSED ITS ATTENTION ON ANTIWAR ACTIVISM. IT ORGANIZED A **PROTEST MARCH** IN WASHINGTON, D.C., ON APRIL 17, 1965, WHICH ATTRACTED 25,000 PARTICIPANTS.

THE WAR'S ESCALATION GALVANIZED CAMPUSES ACROSS THE COUNTRY AND BY 1966 THE SDS AND OTHER STUDENT ACTIVIST GROUPS, DUBBED THE **"NEW LEFT"** BY THE MEDIA, SPONSORED MARCHES AND DEMONSTRATIONS THROUGHOUT THE NATION. NUMEROUS **PASSIVE PROTESTS** INCLUDED STUDENT "SIT-INS" AND "TEACH-INS," IN WHICH CLASSES WERE BOYCOTTED AND CLASSROOMS AND AUDITORIUMS WERE USED AS PLACES FOR DISCUSSIONS ABOUT THE WAR.

THE IMAGES OF **CARNAGE** AND THE EMOTIONALLY CHARGED STORIES FROM TELEVISION REPORTERS IN SOUTH VIETNAM APPEARED TO **EXPOSE** THE GOVERNMENT'S ASSURANCE OF IMMINENT VICTORY AS A **LIE.**

INSTEAD OF STEPPING FORWARD AND EXERCISING FORCEFUL **LEADERSHIP**, PRESIDENT JOHNSON ORDERED GENERAL WESTMORELAND AND OTHER GENERALS IN SOUTH VIETNAM TO **EXPLAIN** TO THE PUBLIC WHAT HAD HAPPENED.

BUT THE **PUBLIC** WANTED TO HEAR FROM THEIR **PRESIDENT.** WHEN THEY DIDN'T, HIS **SILENCE** SEEMED TO CONFIRM THEIR WORST **FEARS** ABOUT THE WAR.

THE MOST IMPORTANT **UNIFYING FACTOR** WAS THE DRAFT, WHICH HUNG OVER THE LIVES OF ALL MALE COLLEGE STUDENTS BECAUSE COLLEGE DRAFT DEFERMENTS ONLY DELAYED, THEY DID NOT ELIMINATE, MILITARY SERVICE. AS THE WAR BECAME MORE UNPOPULAR, MORE AND MORE YOUNG MEN JOINED THE ANTIWAR MOVEMENT.

THOUGH MOST DEMONSTRATIONS WERE PEACEFUL, INEVITABLY THERE WERE OUTBREAKS OF **VIOLENCE** BETWEEN PROTESTORS AND POLICE. INEVITABLE, TOO, WAS THE **RADICALIZATION** OF SOME GROUPS, MOST NOTABLY THE **WEATHERMEN** (LATER KNOWN AS THE WEATHER UNDERGROUND ORGANIZATION), WHICH ADVOCATED MILITANT ACTION AIMED AT A REVOLUTIONARY OVERTHROW OF THE GOVERNMENT. IT FOLLOWED WORDS WITH ACTIONS, INCLUDING THE **"DAYS OF RAGE"** VIOLENT RIOTS IN CHICAGO IN 1969, AND AN ATTEMPT IN 1970 TO BOMB FORT DIX, WHICH FAILED.

THE STUDENT PROTEST MOVEMENT ATTRACTED RESPECTED, **MAINSTREAM AMERICANS** AS WELL. THE INFLUENTIAL PEDIATRICIAN AND BESTSELLING AUTHOR DR. BENJAMIN SPOCK AND THE NOVELIST NORMAN MAILER WERE AMONG THOSE WHO ATTENDED THE FIRST TEACH-IN AT THE UNIVERSITY OF MICHIGAN. TOGETHER WITH OTHER RESPECTED PEOPLE AS WELL AS NUMEROUS LOCAL POLITICIANS AND ACADEMICS DISILLUSIONED WITH THE WAR, THEY LENT THEIR VOICES TO THE RISING PROTEST MOVEMENT.

ON FEBRUARY 27, 1968, THE **JOINT CHIEFS OF STAFF** REQUESTED AN ADDITIONAL **206,000 TROOPS** FOR DEPLOYMENT IN **SOUTH VIETNAM** AND OTHER LOCATIONS, BRINGING THE TOTAL TO ALMOST 700,000 MEN.

TO THE AVERAGE AMERICAN, **EVENTS** IN SOUTH VIETNAM SEEMED INDEED TO BE GOING TO **HELL** IN A HANDBASKET.

UP TO THAT TIME, **ANTIWAR SENTIMENT** HAD BEEN CARRIED BY A **VOCAL MINORITY.** NOW, MORE AND MORE AMERICANS WERE TURNING AGAINST THE WAR.

THE NORTH VIETNAMESE LEADERS SOON DISCOVERED THAT THOUGH THEY HAD SUFFERED A CRUSHING DEFEAT ON THE **BATTLEFIELD**, THEY HAD ACHIEVED A STRATEGIC VICTORY ON THE **POLITICAL FRONT.** AMERICA'S WILL TO CONTINUE THE WAR HAD BEEN **BROKEN.**

AS DISASTROUS AS AMERICANS THOUGHT THE TET OFFENSIVE WAS, ANOTHER INCIDENT IN 1968 **ENRAGED** THE NATION FURTHER. ON MARCH 16, COMPANY C, 1ST BATTALION, 20TH INFANTRY, 11TH INFANTRY BRIGADE, 23RD (AMERICAL) DIVISION BOARDED ITS HELICOPTERS IN SUPPORT OF **OPERATION WHEELER/WALLOWA.**

ITS **MISSION** WAS TO CONDUCT A SEARCH-AND-DESTROY **SWEEP** THROUGH AN AREA ABOUT 80 MILES SOUTHEAST OF DA NANG IN **QUANG NGAI PROVINCE.** AT 7:30 A.M., THE HELICOPTERS TOOK OFF FOR THEIR OBJECTIVE--A CLUSTER OF **FOUR HAMLETS.**

THE TROOPS CALLED THE GROUP OF HAMLETS **"PINKVILLE"** BECAUSE THE LOCALS WERE KNOWN TO BE SYMPATHETIC TO THE 48TH VIETCONG LOCAL FORCE BATTALION BASED IN THE AREA.

COMMANDING COMPANY C WAS **CAPTAIN ERNEST MEDINA.** HIS SUBORDINATE, AND COMMANDER OF THE FIRST PLATOON, WAS **1ST LIEUTENANT WILLIAM CALLEY.**

THE SOLDIERS HAD BEEN TOLD ANYONE THEY ENCOUNTERED WOULD BE THE **ENEMY.** INTELLIGENCE HAD ESTIMATED THAT AS MANY AS **250 VIETCONG** WERE OPERATING IN THE AREA.

WITH HELICOPTER GUNSHIPS PROVIDING SUPPORT AND **COVER,** COMPANY C DISEMBARKED, FANNED OUT, AND BEGAN ITS **ADVANCE** TOWARD THE HAMLET NAMED **MY LAI 4.**

THE MEDIA IN THE VIETNAM WAR, PART 2

THE VIETNAM WAR BECAME KNOWN AS THE WORLD'S FIRST **"TELEVISION WAR"** AS A RESULT OF THE REPORTS BROADCAST DAILY ON THE NETWORK NIGHTLY NEWS PROGRAMS.

TELEVISION REPLACED THE **MOVIE NEWSREELS** OF EARLIER WARS AND BROUGHT THE STORY OF THE VIETNAM CONFLICT INTO AMERICAN HOMES--AND, IN THE 24 PERCENT OF HOUSEHOLDS THAT HAD COLOR TELEVISIONS IN 1968, **IN LIVING COLOR.** IN A 1976 STUDY, PROFESSOR GEORGE BAILEY OF THE UNIVERSITY OF WISCONSIN CONCLUDED THAT THE NETWORKS AIRED ABOUT **184 HOURS** OF NEWS ABOUT THE VIETNAM WAR FROM 1965 TO 1970, AN AVERAGE OF ABOUT THREE MINUTES PER NETWORK PER NIGHT.

TELEVISION COVERAGE OF THE TET OFFENSIVE REVEALED THE ENORMOUS **POWER** OF THE MEDIUM. FOOTAGE OF THE BLOOD AND CARNAGE OF BATTLE WERE HORRIBLE ENOUGH. THEN CAME THE IMAGE OF SOUTH VIETNAMESE NATIONAL POLICE GENERAL NGUYEN NGOC LOAN'S SUMMARY EXECUTION OF AN UNARMED, HANDCUFFED PRISONER ON A BATTLE-SCARRED STREET IN SAIGON. IT DEEPLY **SHOCKED** THE NATION...AND THE REST OF THE WORLD.

A LATER REPORT ON THE EXECUTION REVEALED THAT THE PRISONER WAS A VIETCONG DEATH SQUAD LEADER WHO HAD EARLIER PRESIDED OVER THE **EXECUTIONS** OF AS MANY AS 34 SOUTH VIETNAMESE POLICE

AT **LUNCH TIME**, CAPTAIN MEDINA ORDERED HIS MEN TO TAKE A BREAK AND **EAT.**

AT THE END OF THE DAY, COMPANY C RETURNED TO BASE, ITS **MISSION ACCOMPLISHED.**

OFFICERS AND THEIR FAMILIES, INCLUDING A CLOSE FRIEND OF LOAN'S. BY THE TIME THIS WAS KNOWN, AMERICAN SOCIETY HAD ALREADY PASSED THE TIPPING POINT ON ITS VIEW OF THE WAR, AND THAT AWFUL IMAGE OF "STREET JUSTICE" WAS A PROPELLING FORCE.

TELEVISION COVERAGE DURING THE TET OFFENSIVE SPARKED MUCH **CRITICISM,** THE MOST EXTREME CLAIM BEING THAT IT CAUSED AMERICA TO **LOSE** THE WAR IN VIETNAM. MORE COMMON CHARGES WERE TELEVISION'S TENDENCY TOWARD **SENSATIONALISM,** AND DURING 1968 AND LATER, AN **ANTIWAR BIAS.** THE SUBJECT IS ONE THAT AROUSES MUCH PASSION EVEN TO THIS DAY.

PART OF THIS **CONTROVERSY** AROSE FROM THE NATURE OF THE MEDIUM ITSELF. WHERE IT WAS MOST **EFFECTIVE** WAS IN ITS ABILITY TO SHOW VIVIDLY THE IMMEDIATE **COST** OF WAR. WHERE TELEVISION COVERAGE WAS **WEAK,** PARTICULARLY DURING THE TET OFFENSIVE, WAS IN ANALYSIS THAT COULD COUNTERBALANCE OR PUT INTO **PERSPECTIVE** THE DRAMATIC FOOTAGE BEING AIRED. THERE WERE MANY REASONS FOR THIS, NOT THE LEAST OF WHICH WAS **LOGISTICS.** JUST GETTING THE RAW, UNPROCESSED FILM FOOTAGE FROM SAIGON TO NETWORK OFFICES IN NEW YORK, AND GETTING IT AIRED IN A TIMELY FASHION, WAS DAUNTING.

EVEN THOUGH HE REPEATEDLY THOUGHT ABOUT PLACING **RESTRICTIONS** ON REPORTERS, AT NO TIME DURING THE VIETNAM WAR DID GENERAL WESTMORELAND IMPOSE PRESS CENSORSHIP.

ALMOST IMMEDIATELY, RUMORS OF **ATROCITIES** AT MY LAI 4 BEGAN TO CIRCULATE AMONG MILITARY BASES IN SOUTH VIETNAM. THE BRIGADE HAD A NOTORIOUS REPUTATION FOR **POOR DISCIPLINE** AND WEAK LEADERSHIP, AND SOME UNITS WITHIN IT WERE DESCRIBED AS BEING LITTLE MORE THAN ORGANIZED BANDS OF **THUGS.**

20th INFANTRY 1ST BRIGADE

AN **INVESTIGATION** INTO THE EVENTS OF MARCH 16 WAS INITIATED TWO DAYS AFTER THE OPERATION. MYSTERIOUSLY, **NOTHING** CAME OF IT.

ROBERT RIDENHOUR, A COMBAT INFAN-TRYMAN, HEARD THE RUMORS AND WAS SHOCKED BY THEM. HE BEGAN HIS OWN **INVESTIGATION.** ON MARCH 29, 1969, AFTER HE HAD LEFT THE SERVICE, AND MORE THAN A YEAR AFTER THE INCIDENT, RIDENHOUR WROTE **25 LETTERS** TO THE WHITE HOUSE AND CONGRESS RECOUNT-ING HIS **FINDINGS.**

AT THE **INSISTENCE** OF SOME MEMBERS OF CONGRESS, **TWO INVESTIGATIONS** WERE LAUNCHED. ONE WAS CONDUCTED BY THE **ARMY CRIMINAL INVESTIGATION DIVISION.** THE SECOND WAS A BOARD OF INQUIRY HEADED BY **LT. GENERAL WILLIAM PEERS.**

PEERS, A WORLD WAR II VETERAN WHO HAD SERVED AS THE COMMANDING OFFICER OF THE 4TH DIVISION IN VIETNAM, HAD A REPUTATION FOR FAIRNESS AND **OBJECTIVITY.** WORKING AN AVERAGE OF SIX DAYS A WEEK FOR FOUR MONTHS, HE **LISTENED** TO 398 WITNESSES AND COMPILED 20,000 PAGES OF TESTIMONY. AS PART OF THE INVESTIGATION HE **VISITED** MY LAI 4 WITH HIS STAFF.

THERE THEY **DISCOVERED** DETAILS OF MASSACRE, RAPE, AND OTHER **ATROCITIES.** ANYWHERE FROM 200 TO 500 CIVILIANS HAD BEEN **KILLED.** THE INCIDENT WAS LATER CALLED THE MOST **NOTORIOUS** AND **DISGRACEFUL ACT** IN U.S. ARMY HISTORY.

THE FOUR-VOLUME **PEERS INQUIRY REPORT,** SUBMITTED ON MARCH 14, 1970, WAS A **DAMNING DOCUMENT.** IT COVERED NOT JUST THE EVENTS AT MY LAI 4 -- IT ALSO INCLUDED AN **INDICTMENT** OF ARMY LEADERSHIP IN THE DIVISION AT EVERY LEVEL FROM THE DIVISION COMMANDER DOWN TO ITS JUNIOR OFFICERS. CHARGES INCLUDED **WAR CRIMES,** COVER-UP, AND DERELICTION OF DUTY. THIRTY OFFICERS WERE FOUND CULPABLE. FOURTEEN WERE FORMALLY CHARGED.

ONLY ONE, **LT. WILLIAM CALLEY,** WAS TRIED AND CONVICTED, IN NOVEMBER 1970, OF MURDERING 22 CIVILIANS. HE WAS SENTENCED TO **LIFE IMPRISONMENT.** THE SENTENCE WAS REDUCED ON APPEAL TO 20 YEARS AND LATER TO 10 YEARS BY THE SECRETARY OF THE ARMY. IN 1974, CALLEY WAS **PAROLED** BY PRESIDENT NIXON.

AMERICANS ACROSS THE COUNTRY WERE SHOCKED AND **SICKENED** BY THE NEWS OF THE EVENT AND TRIAL. TO ALMOST ALL, THE **ATROCITY** AT MY LAI 4 EPITOMIZED EVERYTHING **WRONG** WITH THE VIETNAM WAR.

THE STUDENT-DRIVEN ANTIWAR MOVEMENT GAINED WIDER PUBLIC PARTICIPATION ONCE THE ROLLING THUNDER BOMBING CAMPAIGN STARTED IN FEBRUARY 1965. THE STUDENTS FOR A DEMOCRATIC SOCIETY MARCH ON WASHINGTON, D.C., TO **PROTEST** THE WAR DREW A TURNOUT FAR EXCEEDING THE EXPECTATIONS OF THE ORGANIZERS.

ANOTHER SIGNIFICANT **EVENT** EARLY IN THE ANTIWAR MOVEMENT WAS THE **"VIETNAM DAY"** SYMPOSIUM HELD ON THE CAMPUS OF THE UNIVERSITY OF CALIFORNIA AT BERKELEY IN OCTOBER 1965. THOUSANDS ATTENDED TO DEBATE THE MORAL BASIS OF THE WAR.

JOIN SDS

ONE OF THE **PIVOTAL EVENTS** IN THE ANTIWAR MOVEMENT WAS THE "SPRING MOBILIZATION TO END THE WAR IN VIETNAM"--CALLED "THE MOBE"--THAT WAS HELD IN SAN FRANCISCO AND NEW YORK CITY ON APRIL 15, 1967.

END THE DRAFT LET YOUNG MEN LIVE

END THE WAR NOW

NO MORE

GET US OUT OF VIETNAM

ORGANIZERS INCLUDED THE ACTIVISTS A. J. MUSTE, DAVE DELLINGER, ROBERT GREENBLATT, EDWARD KEATING, SIDNEY PECK, AND, FROM THE SOUTHERN CHRISTIAN LEADERSHIP CONFERENCE, JAMES BEVEL. THE LEADERS CHOSE TO STAGE RALLIES IN **TWO CITIES** IN THE HOPE OF DRAWING CROWDS LARGE ENOUGH TO HAVE AN IMPACT ON WASHINGTON.

THE EVENT IN **NEW YORK CITY** BEGAN IN THE SHEEP MEADOW OF CENTRAL PARK. ESTIMATES VARY, BUT AT LEAST 200,000 AND POSSIBLY AS MANY AS **400,000 PEOPLE**, FROM ALL WALKS OF LIFE AND HOLDING DIFFERENT POLITICAL BELIEFS, ATTENDED. **SPEAKERS** INCLUDED DR. BENJAMIN SPOCK, PETE SEEGER, AND STOKELY CARMICHAEL. THE KEYNOTE SPEAKER WAS CIVIL RIGHTS LEADER **DR. MARTIN LUTHER KING, JR.**

IN **SAN FRANCISCO**, THE EVENT DREW AT LEAST 50,000 AND POSSIBLY AS MANY AS 75,000 PEOPLE. PROMINENT SPEAKERS AT THIS EVENT WERE **CIVIL RIGHTS LEADERS** CORETTA SCOTT KING-- DR. KING'S WIFE--AND JULIAN BOND, AND JOURNALIST ROBERT SCHEER.

DR. KING'S APPEARANCE IN NEW YORK WAS PARTICULARLY **IMPORTANT.** HIS PRESENCE LINKED THE CIVIL RIGHTS AND ANTIWAR MOVEMENTS. HE PROTESTED THE WAR ON **MORAL GROUNDS** AND THE FACT THAT IT TOOK RESOURCES AWAY FROM **DOMESTIC PROGRAMS.**

THE SPRING MOBILIZATION TURNOUT DEMONSTRATED THAT THE **ANTI- WAR MOVEMENT** HAD SHIFTED FROM COLLEGE-CAMPUS ACTIVISM TO SOMETHING REPRESENTATIVE OF **MAINSTREAM AMERICA.**

DAILY·NEWS

RESISTANCE TO DRAFT GROWING
22 ARRESTED IN PROTEST

The Philadelphia Inquirer

PUBLIC SUPPORT OF THE WAR FALTE

PRESIDENT JOHNSON CALLS IN ADV

THE WALL STREET JOURNAL.

RESISTANCE TO WAR GROWS

JOHNSON REJECTS CHARGE OF S.P.C.A.

AMERICAN SUPPORT FOR THE WAR **ERODED** STEADILY IN 1967. BY OCTOBER, A **PUBLIC OPINION POLL** REPORTED THAT 46 PERCENT OF AMERICANS BELIEVED THE WAR IN VIETNAM TO BE A **MISTAKE.**

THE TET OFFENSIVE CAUSED CBS NEWS ANCHORMAN **WALTER CRONKITE**, THE MOST RESPECTED MAN IN TELEVISION NEWS, TO **VISIT** SOUTH VIETNAM HIMSELF TO DISCOVER WHAT WAS HAPPENING.

MAINSTREAM AMERICANS HELD HIM IN SUCH **HIGH ESTEEM** THAT HE WAS AFFECTIONATELY CALLED **"UNCLE WALTER."** ON FEBRUARY 27, 1968, HE REPORTED ON HIS NIGHTLY BROADCAST THAT **TET** HAD BEEN AN AMERICAN **DEFEAT.**

THE ONLY RATIONAL WAY OUT WILL BE TO NEGOTIATE...

...NOT AS VICTORS, BUT AS AN HONORABLE PEOPLE.

AFTER THE **BROADCAST,** JOHNSON TURNED TO HIS PRESS SECRETARY, GEORGE CHRISTIAN.

IF I'VE LOST CRONKITE, I'VE **LOST** MIDDLE AMERICA.

THIS **SHIFT** DEEPLY AFFECTED PRESIDENT JOHNSON. ON MARCH 31, 1968, HE APPEARED ON NATIONAL TV AND MADE A NEW **APPEAL** FOR PEACE IN SOUTHEAST ASIA. BUT MOST PEOPLE ONLY REMEMBER HIS SPEECH'S **CONCLUSION.**

I SHALL NOT SEEK, AND I WILL **NOT ACCEPT,** THE NOMINATION OF MY PARTY FOR **ANOTHER TERM** AS YOUR PRESIDENT.

JOHNSON'S **DECISION** TURNED THE 1968 PRESIDENTIAL CAMPAIGN INTO A **POLITICAL FREE-FOR-ALL.** FOR THE DEMOCRATIC PARTY, THERE WERE **THREE FRONT-RUNNERS.**

VICE PRESIDENT **HUBERT H. HUM-PHREY,** WHO BEGAN HIS CAMPAIGN IN SUP-PORT OF THE WAR.

SENATOR EUGENE **MCCARTHY,** THE ONLY OPENLY ANTI-WAR CANDIDATE.

THE NEED NOW IS FOR A GREAT **RECONCILIATION.**

THE CHALLENGE IS **URGENT.** THE TASK IS **LARGE.** THE TIME IS **NOW.**

AND **SENATOR ROBERT F. KENNEDY,** YOUNGER BROTHER OF THE LATE PRESIDENT.

THE TOP **REPUBLICAN CHALLENGER** WAS FORMER VICE PRESIDENT **RICHARD NIXON,** WHO REPEATEDLY STATED THAT HE HAD A **"SECRET PLAN"** TO END THE WAR IN VIETNAM. YEARS LATER, HE ADMITTED THAT NO SUCH PLAN EVER **EXISTED.**

THIS COUNTRY IS ON A **PERILOUS COURSE.**

EVERY AMERICAN WANTS **PEACE** IN VIETNAM. THE QUESTION IS **WHAT KIND** OF PEACE?

A POWERFUL **THIRD-PARTY CANDIDATE** EMERGED: ALABAMA **GOVERNOR GEORGE WALLACE.** WALLACE HAD MADE A NAME FOR HIMSELF AS A **FOE** OF CIVIL RIGHTS.

HE ANNOUNCED THAT HE WOULD RUN A **"LAW AND ORDER"** PRESIDENTIAL CAMPAIGN. AND HE PROPOSED TO **ESCALATE** THE WAR IN ORDER TO WIN IT QUICKLY AND DECISIVELY.

THE VIETNAM WAR IS THE **MOST IMPORTANT MATTER** FACING THE AMERICAN PEOPLE.

HIS **RUNNING MATE** WAS RETIRED AIR FORCE GENERAL **CURTIS LEMAY**-- WHO IN 1965 HAD ADVOCATED NUKING NORTH VIETNAM BACK TO THE STONE AGE.

THE TWIN FORCES OF THE **VIETNAM WAR** AND **THE CIVIL RIGHTS MOVEMENT** CREATED A PERFECT STORM OVER THE AMERICAN POLITICAL LANDSCAPE. AMERICA EXPERIENCED ITS GREATEST POLITICAL AND SOCIAL **CRISIS** SINCE THE CIVIL WAR.

DEBATE AND RHETORIC, ONCE IMPASSIONED BUT REASONED, BECAME INCREASINGLY **POLARIZED AND ACRIMONIOUS**--AND, IN PLACES ACROSS THE COUNTRY, OVERWHELMED BY **VIOLENCE**.

ON APRIL 4, 1968, DR. MARTIN LUTHER KING, JR., WAS **ASSASSINATED** IN MEMPHIS, TENNESSEE.

TWO MONTHS LATER, ON JUNE 5, 1968, AFTER WINNING THE CALIFORNIA DEMOCRATIC PRIMARY, ROBERT F. KENNEDY WAS **GUNNED DOWN**.

MORE VIOLENCE WAS TO COME.

97

THE **DEMOCRATIC NATIONAL CONVENTION** TO NOMINATE ITS PRESIDENTIAL CANDIDATE WAS SCHEDULED TO OPEN IN **CHICAGO** ON AUGUST 26, 1968. EVEN BEFORE THE CONVENTION BEGAN, ANTI-WAR ACTIVISTS HAD STAGED **PROTESTS** IN THE CITY.

MAYOR RICHARD DALEY, A DEMOCRAT AND ONE OF THE LAST OF THE URBAN **POLITICAL BOSSES**, PROMISED THE CONVENTION THAT THE CITY WOULD MAINTAIN **LAW AND ORDER**.

THE CONVENTION SITE BECAME A **FORTRESS**, WITH CHECKPOINTS, ARMED GUARDS, ARMORED VEHICLES, AND **BARBED-WIRE FENCES**. MAYOR DALEY REQUESTED, AND RECEIVED, REINFORCEMENTS OF ILLINOIS STATE TROOPERS AND **TROOPS** FROM THE ILLINOIS NATIONAL GUARD.

CHICAGO, THE **SECOND LARGEST CITY** IN THE UNITED STATES, RESEMBLED A CITY UNDER **SIEGE**.

HUBERT HUMPHREY **WON** THE NOMINATION AS THE DEMOCRATS' PRESIDENTIAL CANDIDATE. BUT THE **REAL STORY** WAS WHAT WAS HAPPENING **OUTSIDE** THE CONVENTION HALLS.

NEWSPAPERS, RADIO, AND TELEVISION REPORTS DOCUMENTED INSTANCES OF **POLICE VIOLENCE** AGAINST THE ACTIVISTS. THE POLICE MADE 668 ARRESTS--THE LIST EVEN INCLUDED JOURNALISTS.

AMONG THE DEMONSTRATORS WAS CHARISMATIC ANTIESTABLISHMENT REBEL **ABBIE HOFFMAN**, COFOUNDER OF THE YOUTH INTERNATIONAL PARTY (THE SELF-TERMED YIPPIES), WHICH HAD NOMINATED A **PIG** AS THEIR PRESIDENTIAL CANDIDATE.

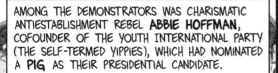

HOFFMAN WAS ONE OF THE **CHICAGO EIGHT** WHO WERE SUBSEQUENTLY PUT ON **TRIAL** FOR A NUMBER OF FEDERAL CHARGES, INCLUDING CONSPIRACY TO CROSS STATE LINES WITH INTENT TO CAUSE A **RIOT.**

THE TRIAL WAS **RAUCOUS**. THE DEFENDANTS CONSTANTLY DISRUPTED PROCEEDINGS AND TRIED TO MAKE THE VIETNAM WAR, RACISM, AND POLITICAL REPRESSION THE **REAL ISSUES**. ADDITIONAL CHARGES OF 175 COUNTS OF **CONTEMPT OF COURT** WERE LEVIED BY THE JUDGE.

APPEALS OVERTURNED ALL CRIMINAL CONVICTIONS, AND EVENTUALLY MOST OF THE CONTEMPT CHARGES WERE **DISMISSED**.

NIXON **WON** THE **REPUBLICAN NOMINATION**, EASILY DEFEATING HIS TWO RIVALS, NEW YORK GOVERNOR NELSON ROCKEFELLER AND CALIFORNIA GOVERNOR **RONALD REAGAN**.

WE'RE ON THE **WRONG ROAD** AND IT'S TIME TO TAKE A **NEW ROAD** TO PROGRESS.

THE **THREE-WAY RACE** FOR THE PRESIDENCY WAS ONE OF THE MOST **CONTENTIOUS** IN AMERICAN HISTORY. THE POPULAR VOTE WAS SURPRISINGLY **CLOSE**: NIXON GOT 43.4 PERCENT, HUMPHREY GOT 42.7 PERCENT, AND WALLACE GOT 13.5 PERCENT.

BUT NIXON'S **ELECTORAL COLLEGE TRIUMPH** WAS DECISIVE: 301 VOTES COMPARED TO 191 FOR HUMPHREY AND 46 FOR WALLACE.

100

MEANWHILE, THERE WAS A **CHANGING OF THE GUARD** IN SOUTH VIETNAM AS WELL. IN JULY 1968, PRESIDENT JOHNSON RECALLED GENERAL WESTMORELAND FROM SOUTH VIETNAM AND APPOINTED HIM **U.S. ARMY CHIEF OF STAFF.**

GENERAL CREIGHTON ABRAMS, WESTMORELAND'S FORMER DEPUTY, OFFICIALLY BECAME THE **NEW HEAD** OF MACV ON JULY 3. NO ONE ENVIED HIM.

BUT ABRAMS HAD STUDIED **ENEMY TACTICS** IN WAYS THAT WESTMORELAND HADN'T. NOW THAT HE WAS IN **COMMAND,** HE COULD PUT HIS **KNOWLEDGE** TO USE.

ABRAMS **DISCARDED** WESTMORELAND'S **SEARCH-AND-DESTROY TACTICS** AND BODY COUNT MEASURES. HE **INTEGRATED** THE SEPARATE COMBAT, PACIFICATION, AND ARVN SUPPORT OPERATIONS INTO WHAT HE CALLED A **"ONE WAR"** CONCEPT.

ABRAMS ALSO **REDUCED** THE NUMBER OF MASSIVE TROOP SWEEPS, BELIEVING THEY WERE **INEFFECTIVE**.

INSTEAD, HE ORDERED AN **INCREASE** IN SMALL-UNIT PATROLS AND **AMBUSHES**. HE BELIEVED THAT THESE WOULD DO A **BETTER JOB** OF KEEPING THE COMMUNISTS OUT OF THE VILLAGES.

HE ALSO STEPPED UP **SMALL-UNIT ATTACKS** ON THE COMMUNISTS' LOGISTICS **INFRASTRUCTURE**.

FOR THE **FIRST TIME** IN THE WAR, THE ENEMY'S TRADITIONAL BASES OF POWER ARE BEING DIRECTLY **CHALLENGED**.

BOTH SIDES ARE NOW FIGHTING THE **SAME WAR**.

MEANWHILE, IN PARIS, WHERE **PEACE NEGOTIATIONS** HAD FINALLY BEGUN, THE NORTH VIETNAMESE HAD BEEN **MONITORING** THE AMERICAN PRESIDENTIAL CAMPAIGN AND HOPING FOR A **HUMPHREY VICTORY.**

THEY BELIEVED THEY COULD GET A **BETTER DEAL** FROM HIM THAN FROM NIXON, WHO HAD A LONG-STANDING "TOUGH ON COMMUNISM" REPUTATION.

ACCORDINGLY, DISCUSSIONS, WHICH BECAME **INFAMOUS** FOR THE LITANY OF COMMUNIST DEMANDS AND HARD-LINE POSITIONS--INCLUDING THE **REJECTION** OF SOUTH VIETNAMESE GOVERNMENT REPRESENTATIVES--HAD "BREAKTHROUGHS" THAT WERE SUBTLY TIMED TO **BENEFIT** THE DEMOCRATS.

WHEN NIXON WON AND BECAME THE **37TH PRESIDENT** OF THE UNITED STATES, THE NORTH VIETNAMESE **REASSESSED** THEIR STRATEGY.

THE DEMANDS BECAME MORE **OBDURATE.** THEY INSISTED THAT NIXON **DISSOLVE** THE SAIGON GOVERNMENT, **DISBAND** THE SOUTH VIETNAMESE ARMY, AND INSTALL A **NEW COALITION** EMPOWERED TO NEGOTIATE A **TRUCE.**

PRESIDENT NIXON WAS UNDER **ENORMOUS PRESSURE.** THE MOST VOCAL DOMESTIC OPPONENTS OF THE WAR DEMANDED AN **IMMEDIATE PULLOUT.** ON NOVEMBER 3, 1969, HE ADDRESSED THE AMERICAN PEOPLE.

THE **QUESTION** AT ISSUE IS NOT WHETHER JOHNSON'S WAR BECOMES NIXON'S WAR.

THE GREAT QUESTION IS: HOW CAN WE WIN **AMERICA'S** PEACE?

THE **OBSTACLE** IS THE OTHER SIDE'S ABSOLUTE **REFUSAL** TO SHOW THE LEAST WILLINGNESS TO JOIN US IN SEEKING A **JUST PEACE.**

PRESIDENT NIXON ELABORATED ON THE **PROBLEMS** HE FACED AND THE SOLUTIONS HE **PROPOSED.**

KNOWN AS NIXON'S "SILENT MAJORITY SPEECH," IT ANNOUNCED A NEW POLICY, **VIETNAMIZATION.** SOUTH VIETNAM WOULD BECOME RESPONSIBLE FOR CONTINUING THE WAR.

AND SO TONIGHT, TO YOU, THE GREAT **SILENT MAJORITY** OF MY FELLOW AMERICANS, I ASK FOR YOUR **SUPPORT.**

104

PART FOUR:
VIETNAMIZATION

HO CHI MINH, THE LONGTIME PRESIDENT OF NORTH VIETNAM, WHO HAD BECOME A SYMBOL OF THE COMMUNIST PARTY IN VIETNAM AND OF VIETNAMESE UNIFICATION, **DIED** ON SEPTEMBER 2, 1969. THREE DAYS BEFORE HIS DEATH, HE REJECTED A **PEACE OFFER** FROM PRESIDENT NIXON AND REITERATED THE NORTH'S **UNCOMPROMISING POSITION** REGARDING TOTAL INCORPORATION OF SOUTH VIETNAM UNDER THE NORTH'S FLAG.

NOW OTHERS IN THE NORTH VIETNAMESE POLITBURO WOULD CONTINUE THE **STRUGGLE**, THOUGH NO ONE COULD PREDICT WHEN IT WOULD END.

BUT THE COMMUNISTS HAD THE WILL TO **WAIT.** AMERICANS DID NOT. IT WAS A MEASURE OF HOW FAR THE WAR HAD **FRACTURED** AMERICAN SOCIETY THAT PRESIDENT NIXON'S NEW POLICY OF **VIETNAMIZATION** WAS SEEN BY SOME AS BETTER LATE THAN NEVER, BY OTHERS AS TOO LATE TO MAKE A DIFFERENCE, AND WAS REJECTED OUTRIGHT BY STILL OTHERS WHO WANTED AMERICA OUT OF VIETNAM, REGARDLESS OF COST AND **CONSEQUENCES.**

IN TRUTH, NO ONE KNEW FOR SURE WHAT THE **ENDGAME** WOULD BE.

PRESIDENT NIXON KNEW THAT AN **IMMEDIATE PULLOUT** OF VIETNAM WAS NOT A REALISTIC OPTION. HE HAD TO SOLVE A NUMBER OF PROBLEMS BEFORE A PULLOUT WAS POSSIBLE.

ONE OF THE MOST INTRACTABLE AND **TRAGIC** PROBLEMS WAS THE FATE OF AMERICAN PRISONERS OF WAR--**POWS**--HELD BY THE COMMUNISTS.

BECAUSE THE U.S. CONGRESS HAD NEVER DECLARED **WAR** ON NORTH VIETNAM, HANOI CLAIMED THE CAPTURED AMERICANS, MOSTLY **AVIATORS**, WERE NOT PROTECTED BY THE **GENEVA CONVENTIONS**.

INSTEAD, HANOI LABELED THEM **CRIMINALS** AND CALLED THEM "YANKEE AIR PIRATES" WHO HAD COMMITTED **ATROCITIES** AGAINST THE PEOPLE OF NORTH VIETNAM.

THE NORTH VIETNAMESE SET ASIDE **11 PRISONS** FOR THE POWS. FOUR WERE IN HANOI. THE POWS GAVE THEM ALL **NICKNAMES**, SUCH AS DOGPATCH, THE PLANTATION, AND DIRTY BIRD. THE MOST INFAMOUS WAS HOA LOA PRISON, WHICH THE AMERICANS CALLED THE **HANOI HILTON**.

THE NORTH VIETNAMESE POLITBURO CALLOUSLY **EXPLOITED** THE PRISONERS, REBUFFING PETITIONS AND **PLEAS** TO PROVIDE A LIST OF NAMES OF CAPTURED AMERICANS. MEANWHILE, THE POWS ENDURED **TORTURE** SO SEVERE THAT, ACCORDING TO SOME ACCOUNTS, AS MANY AS **72 DIED** IN THE PROCESS.

OCCASIONALLY, THE POLITBURO WOULD ARRANGE **MEETINGS** BETWEEN SELECT POWS AND FOREIGN JOURNALISTS FOR **PROPAGANDA PURPOSES.** THE NORTH VIETNAMESE RIGIDLY CONTROLLED THESE MEETINGS. THE PRISONERS WERE TOLD THEY WOULD BE PUNISHED IF THEY **"MISBEHAVED."**

IN MAY 1966, TELEVISION CAMERAS RECORDED **POW NAVY CAPTAIN JEREMIAH DENTON, JR.,** WHOSE EYES KEPT **BLINKING** SPASMODICALLY. SOME THOUGHT IT WAS DUE TO THE HARSH TV CAMERA **LIGHTS.**

IN REALITY, HE WAS BLINKING IN **MORSE CODE:** T - O - R - T - U - R - E.

UNLIKE PRESIDENT JOHNSON, WHO HAD ALL BUT **IGNORED** THE POWS BECAUSE HE COULD DO **NOTHING** TO STOP THEIR **ABUSE**, NIXON DETERMINED TO DO EVERYTHING HE COULD TO **HELP** THEM.

WHEN **DIPLOMATIC PRESSURE** TO IMPROVE THE CONDITIONS OF THEIR CAPTIVITY **FAILED**, NIXON DECIDED TO USE **MILITARY ACTION**. IN 1970, HE AUTHORIZED A DARING PLAN TO **RESCUE** AMERICAN POWS HELD AT **SON TAY PRISON,** JUST 23 MILES WEST OF HANOI.

SON TAY WAS VIRTUALLY IN THE **BACKYARD** OF NORTH VIETNAM'S CAPITAL. IN ADDITION TO FREEING THE POWS, THE MISSION WAS INTENDED TO SEND A **MESSAGE** TO HANOI THAT AMERICA'S MILITARY RESOLVE REMAINED FIRM.

PLANNING BEGAN ON AUGUST 8, 1970. THE RESCUE TEAM WAS LED BY ARMY **COLONEL ARTHUR D. "BULL" SIMONS.**

ON THE NIGHT OF NOVEMBER 20-21, 1970, THE RESCUE ATTEMPT, NOW CODE-NAMED **OPERATION KINGPIN**, WAS LAUNCHED.

IT WAS THE LARGEST AND MOST COMPLEX **SPECIAL OPERATION** OF THE VIETNAM WAR. THREE HELICOPTERS, CARRYING 56 RESCUERS, LANDED IN AND AROUND SON TAY. THEY WERE **SUPPORTED** BY HELICOPTER GUNSHIPS, FIGHTERS, AND OTHER AIRCRAFT. IN ADDITION, THE SEVENTH FLEET STAGED **DIVERSIONARY AIR RAIDS** OVER HANOI AND THE PORT OF HAIPHONG.

THE RESCUERS HAD **26 MINUTES** TO FREE AN ESTIMATED 60 PRISONERS BEFORE COMMUNIST **REINFORCEMENTS** ARRIVED. BUT THEIR EFFORT WAS IN VAIN. THE PRISONERS HAD BEEN MOVED. QUICKLY THE MEN REBOARDED THEIR HELICOPTERS AND HEADED BACK TO THEIR BASES. THE FLIGHT BACK SEEMED TO TAKE FOREVER. THE MEN WERE CONVINCED THEY HAD **FAILED**.

109

INDEED, THE RAID CREATED A **FIRESTORM** OF CONTROVERSY. WHEN NEWS OF KINGPIN WAS MADE PUBLIC, **RECRIMINATIONS** FROM POLITICIANS AND MANY OTHERS DROWNED OUT ANY **PRAISE** FOR THE OPERATION. CONGRESS CONDUCTED **INVESTIGATIONS** INTO THE "INTELLIGENCE FAILURE" REGARDING THE ABSENCE OF PRISONERS AT SON TAY.

BUT PRESIDENT NIXON WAS **PROUD** OF THE MEN WHO HAD CONDUCTED THE SON TAY RAID. IN A PUBLIC CEREMONY, HE **DECORATED** FOUR OF THE MEN INVOLVED. COLONEL SIMONS RECEIVED THE DISTINGUISHED SERVICE CROSS, THE ARMY'S **SECOND-HIGHEST AWARD** FOR VALOR.

IN A LATER CEREMONY, SECRETARY OF DEFENSE MELVIN LAIRD DECORATED **EVERY MAN** WHO HAD PARTICIPATED.

THE RAID DID SUCCEED IN **ONE** IMPORTANT RESPECT. IT **PANICKED** THE NORTH VIETNAMESE POLITBURO, WHO WERE CONVINCED THAT PRESIDENT NIXON PLANNED TO **INVADE** THEIR COUNTRY. FROM THAT POINT ON, **TORTURE** OF POWS **STOPPED** AND TREATMENT OF THEM IMPROVED.

The HO CHI MINH TRAIL

ANOTHER PROBLEM THAT PRESIDENT NIXON WANTED TO SOLVE WAS THE FLOW OF **SUPPLIES** REACHING COMMUNISTS IN THE SOUTH. DURING THE JOHNSON ADMINISTRATION, BOMBING OF THE HO CHI MINH TRAIL WAS RESTRICTED AND, AT TIMES, **FORBIDDEN**...

...EVEN THOUGH THE COMMUNIST SUPPLY ROUTE WAS A **VIOLATION** OF LAOS'S AND CAMBODIA'S **NEUTRALITY**. THE **RULER** OF CAMBODIA, PRINCE NORODOM SIHANOUK, PUBLICLY **REFUSED** TO ALLOW AMERICANS TO BOMB COMMUNIST BASES IN HIS COUNTRY.

NIXON WAS DETERMINED TO **DESTROY** THE COMMUNIST BASES, REGARDLESS. BUT ANY MISSION WOULD HAVE TO BE **TOP SECRET.**

IN EARLY 1969, NIXON AUTHORIZED A MISSION CODE-NAMED **OPERATION MENU.** ITS PURPOSE WAS TO **DESTROY** THE LARGE DEPOTS AND BASE CAMPS ON THE HO CHI MINH TRAIL, AND PREVENT ANOTHER TET OFFENSIVE-LIKE BUILDUP.

THE MISSIONS WERE SO **SECRET** THAT NOT EVEN THE BOMBER CREWS KNEW THE TARGET **LOCATIONS.** GIVEN SETS OF NAVIGATIONAL COORDINATES THAT WOULD TAKE THEM CLOSE TO DESIGNATED TARGETS OVER SOUTH VIETNAM, THE CREWS WERE TOLD THEY WOULD THEN RECEIVE **NEW COORDINATES** FOR THE ACTUAL BOMB RUN.

ON MARCH 18, 1969, THE **FIRST TARGET**, BASE AREA 353 IN CAMBODIA, WAS BOMBED.

THE **COVERT ASPECT** OF THE BOMBING **ENDED** IN MARCH 1970 WHEN PRINCE SIHANOUK WAS DEPOSED AND CAMBODIA'S **NEW LEADER**, GENERAL LON NOL, REQUESTED OUTSIDE **ASSISTANCE** AGAINST THE COMMUNISTS.

ON APRIL 29, 1970, 6,000 SOUTH VIETNAMESE TROOPS SUPPORTED BY AMERICAN AIRCRAFT **LAUNCHED** A **MAJOR ATTACK** AGAINST THE COMMUNIST-HELD REGION IN CAMBODIA KNOWN AS THE **PARROT'S BEAK**.

PRESIDENT NIXON CITED THE **ALLIED VICTORY** AT PARROT'S BEAK AS AN EXAMPLE OF **SUCCESS** IN HIS VIETNAMIZATION PROGRAM.

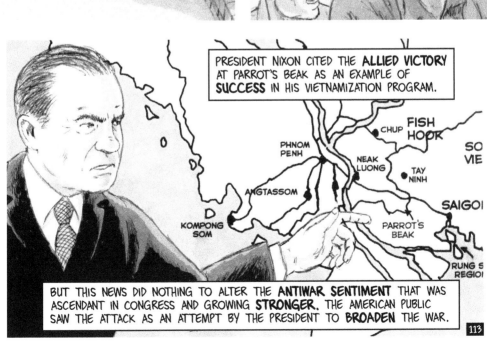

FISH HOOK
CHUP
PHNOM PENH
NEAK LUONG
TAY NINH
SO VIE
ANGTASSOM
SAIGOI
KOMPONG SOM
PARROT'S BEAK
RUNG S REGIOI

BUT THIS NEWS DID NOTHING TO ALTER THE **ANTIWAR SENTIMENT** THAT WAS ASCENDANT IN CONGRESS AND GROWING **STRONGER**. THE AMERICAN PUBLIC SAW THE ATTACK AS AN ATTEMPT BY THE PRESIDENT TO **BROADEN** THE WAR.

TWO STRONG **ANTIWAR ADVOCATES** IN THE SENATE WERE JOHN SHERMAN COOPER OF KENTUCKY (A REPUBLICAN) AND FRANK CHURCH OF IDAHO (A DEMOCRAT). **ANGRY** OVER THE BOMBING CAMPAIGN IN CAMBODIA, THEY WANTED TO **COUNTER** THE EXECUTIVE BRANCH'S "BLANK CHECK" PROVIDED BY THE TONKIN GULF RESOLUTION.

THEY SPONSORED THE **COOPER-CHURCH AMENDMENT** TO THE DEPARTMENT OF DEFENSE BUDGET. IT INCLUDED THE **REVOCATION** OF THE TONKIN GULF RESOLUTION AND PLACED MANY **RESTRICTIONS** ON HOW THE PRESIDENT COULD CONTINUE THE WAR AND SUPPORT OF SOUTH VIETNAM.

THE NIXON ADMINISTRATION **DENOUNCED** THE AMENDMENT, CLAIMING IT HARMED MILITARY EFFORTS AND WEAKENED AMERICA'S **BARGAINING POSITION** AT THE PARIS PEACE TALKS.

THE AMENDMENT **PASSED** IN THE SENATE BY A VOTE OF 58 TO 37, BUT WAS **DEFEATED** IN THE HOUSE BY A VOTE OF 237 TO 153. A **MODIFIED VERSION** OF THE AMENDMENT, ATTACHED TO THE SUPPLEMENTARY FOREIGN ASSISTANCE ACT OF 1970, WAS **PASSED** BY CONGRESS IN LATE DECEMBER AND **ENACTED** IN JANUARY 1971.

THE SOUTH VIETNAMESE ARMY'S **BIG TEST** UNDER THE NEW VIETNAMIZATION STRATEGY WAS **OPERATION LAM SON 719.** ITS PURPOSE WAS TO STOP SOUTHBOUND SUPPLY SHIPMENTS. THE FIRST OBJECTIVE WAS TO CAPTURE THE MAJOR SUPPLY DEPOT AT TCHÉPONE, LAOS. THE SECOND WAS TO SEVER THE HO CHI MINH TRAIL ITSELF.

THE COOPER-CHURCH AMENDMENT NOW PROHIBITED USE OF AMERICAN **GROUND TROOPS** IN LAOS AND CAMBODIA. BUT AMERICAN **MILITARY AIRCRAFT** COULD BE USED. AN ATTACK WAS LAUNCHED ON FEBRUARY 8, 1971.

THE SOUTH VIETNAMESE ARMY DEDICATED 15,000 TROOPS TO THE **TWO-MONTH** CAMPAIGN. AT FIRST, THINGS WENT WELL FOR THE ARVN.

AMERICAN AND SOUTH VIETNAMESE INTELLIGENCE ESTIMATED THAT IT WOULD TAKE NORTH VIETNAM A **MONTH** TO MOVE A DIVISION IN TO SUPPORT THE TROOPS AROUND TCHÉPONE. THE ESTIMATE PROVED TO BE ONE OF THE **BIGGEST ERRORS** IN THE WAR.

115

WITHIN **TWO WEEKS**, NORTH VIETNAM WAS ABLE TO MOVE AS MANY AS **FIVE DIVISIONS**--ALMOST 70,000 MEN--TO THE BATTLEFIELD. THE ARVN GROUND ATTACK STALLED.

LOW CLOUD COVER INHIBITED THE USE OF AMERICAN AIR POWER.

WHEN THE WEATHER **CLEARED**, AIR STRIKES COMMENCED WITH DEADLY EFFICIENCY. BY MARCH 8, TCHÉPONE WAS **CAPTURED** BY ARVN TROOPS AND A SIGNIFICANT NUMBER OF WEAPONS AND SUPPLIES WERE **DESTROYED**. AFTER TWO WEEKS OF OPERATIONS TO FIND AND DESTROY ADDITIONAL CACHES, THE SOUTH VIETNAMESE TROOPS WERE ORDERED TO **RETURN**.

ON APRIL 7, 1971, PRESIDENT NIXON PROUDLY **STATED**...

TONIGHT I CAN REPORT VIETNAMIZATION HAS SUC-CEEDED.

BUT THE VICTORY WAS NOT **CLEAR-CUT**. MANY SOUTH VIETNAMESE ARMY UNITS FOUGHT POORLY, AND SOME PANICKED. ONLY THE MASSIVE **INTERVENTION** OF U.S. AIRPOWER PREVENTED DEFEAT DURING OPERATION LAM SON 719.

IN 1968, AT THE **PEAK** OF AMERICA'S INVOLVEMENT IN THE VIETNAM WAR, THERE WERE MORE THAN **A HALF MILLION** U.S. TROOPS IN SOUTHEAST ASIA.

BY EARLY **1972**, U.S. GROUND TROOP STRENGTH WAS REDUCED TO ABOUT **65,000 MEN**, ALMOST ALL ADVISORS.

THE AMERICAN AIR FORCES HAD SIMILARLY **SHRUNK**. WHERE THOUSANDS OF AIRCRAFT HAD ONCE DEPLOYED, NOW ONLY **800 AIRCRAFT** OF ALL TYPES--FROM B-52s DOWN TO OBSERVATION PLANES--WERE IN SOUTHEAST ASIA.

AS AMERICAN TROOPS LEFT, THEY GAVE SOUTH VIETNAM THEIR **MILITARY HARDWARE** AND SUPPLIES. ON PAPER, SOUTH VIETNAM HAD A STRONG AND **WELL-EQUIPPED** ARMY. BUT TRAINING WAS UNEVEN, AND TROOP MORALE WAS QUESTIONABLE.

MEANWHILE, NORTH VIETNAM HAD THE WORLD'S **FIFTH LARGEST ARMY.** ITS EQUIPMENT WAS **MODERN**; ITS TROOPS WERE TRAINED AND **MOTIVATED.** THE NORTH VIETNAMESE POLITUBURO CHOSE IN LATE 1971 TO USE THESE RESOURCES IN A **DECISIVE BID** TO WIN THE WAR.

DEFENSE MINISTER GENERAL GIAP RECEIVED APPROVAL TO LAUNCH THE **NGUYEN HUE CAMPAIGN.** NAMED AFTER THE LEGENDARY VIETNAMESE HERO, IT WAS A **THREE-PRONG OFFENSIVE:** ACROSS THE DMZ, THROUGH THE CENTRAL HIGHLANDS, AND INTO THE SOUTH.

IT WAS DESIGNED TO STRIKE A **KNOCKOUT BLOW** AGAINST THE SOUTH VIETNAMESE ARMY AND WIN THE WAR. LAUNCH TIME FOR THE OFFENSIVE WAS AFTER THE **MONSOON SEASON** BEGAN, WHEN AMERICAN AIRPOWER WOULD BE GROUNDED BY THE BAD WEATHER.

THE NORTH VIETNAMESE **OFFENSIVE** BEGAN WITH THE NORTHERN PRONG OF THE ATTACK ON MARCH 30, 1972... EASTER WEEKEND. AS A RESULT, AMERICAN TROOPS CALLED IT THE **EASTER OFFENSIVE.** NVA TROOPS FROM THE NORTH ADVANCED SOUTH ACROSS THE **DMZ**, AND EAST FROM BASES IN THE A SHAU VALLEY, TOWARD HUE AND DA NANG.

THREE DAYS LATER, THE SOUTHERNMOST PRONG LAUNCHED THE **SECOND STAGE** OF THE OFFENSIVE FROM BASES IN CAMBODIA, ATTACKING TOWARD SAIGON. THE **THIRD PRONG**, LAUNCHED FROM BASES ALONG THE LAOS-CAMBODIA BORDER, STRUCK THE PROVINCE OF BINH DINH. A TOTAL OF **120,000 TROOPS** AND 1,200 TANKS AND OTHER ARMORED VEHICLES PARTICIPATED IN THE OFFENSIVE.

THE ARVN LEADERSHIP WAS TAKEN BY **SURPRISE.** SOME UNITS RALLIED AND RESISTED VALIANTLY, WHILE OTHERS PANICKED AND **ABANDONED** THEIR POSITIONS. IN SOME CASES, THE NORTH VIETNAMESE CAPTURED INTACT ARTILLERY BATTERIES AND WERE ABLE TO TURN THE CANNONS AROUND AND USE THEM AGAINST THE **ROUTED** ARVN FORCES.

THOUGH GENERAL ABRAMS AND HIS STAFF IN SAIGON RECEIVED REPORTS OF **ENEMY ACTION**, INITIALLY THEY REMAINED **IGNORANT** OF THE STRENGTH AND EXTENT OF THE FIGHTING.

BECAUSE OF THE AMERICAN **TROOP DRAWDOWN**, MOST SOUTH VIETNAMESE ARMY UNITS NO LONGER HAD AMERICAN ADVISORS.

ABRAMS AND HIS STAFF RECEIVED FEW REPORTS, AND MOST WERE VAGUE OR **WILDLY OPTIMISTIC**.

ONLY ON THE **FOURTH DAY** DID GENERAL ABRAMS AND HIS MEN DISCOVER THE **TRUTH.** THE SOUTH VIETNAMESE MILITARY LEADERS HAD REFUSED TO TELL THE FULL STORY BECAUSE THEY WERE **EMBARRASSED** BY THEIR INTELLIGENCE FAILURE...THEY HAD **LOST FACE.**

THOUGH ARVN **RESISTANCE** WAS UNEVEN, SOME UNITS FOUGHT BRAVELY AND WITH GREAT SKILL. AFTER THE **INITIAL SHOCK,** MORE AND MORE ARVN UNITS **DUG IN.**

GENERAL ABRAMS QUICKLY PREPARED AN **AERIAL COUNTER-ATTACK.** DESPITE THE CLOUD COVER, AMERICAN AIRCRAFT WERE ABLE TO USE ELECTRONIC DEVICES TO LOCATE GROUND TARGETS. A HEAVY BOMBING CAMPAIGN, CODE-NAMED **OPERATION LINEBACKER,** WAS LAUNCHED.

THE NORTH VIETNAMESE TROOPS WERE **SURPRISED** BY HOW QUICKLY SOUTH VIETNAMESE UNITS **REBOUNDED** AND HOW WELL THEY **FOUGHT BACK.** INSTEAD OF QUICKLY "LIBERATING" SOUTH VIETNAM, THE EASTER OFFENSIVE **STALLED.**

DURING **BREAKS** IN THE WEATHER, AMERICAN TACTICAL AIR STRIKES WERE **DEVASTATING.**

HARD FIGHTING CONTINUED UNTIL JUNE 1972. THOUGH PARTS OF SOUTH VIETNAM REMAINED IN THE HANDS OF THE NVA, THE CAMPAIGN HAD **FAILED.** SOUTH VIETNAM HAD NOT SURRENDERED. THE NORTH VIETNAMESE ARMY HAD BEEN **DECIMATED.** IT SUFFERED ABOUT 100,000 CASUALTIES. HALF OF THEIR LARGE-CALIBER ARTILLERY AND TANKS WERE **DESTROYED.**

PRESIDENT NIXON'S **TOP NEGOTIATOR** FOR THE PARIS PEACE TALKS WAS NATIONAL SECURITY ADVISOR **DR. HENRY KISSINGER.** KISSINGER HAD BEGUN **SECRET TALKS** WITH THE TOP NORTH VIETNAMESE NEGOTIATOR, LE DUC THO, BACK IN AUGUST 1969.

THOSE SECRET DISCUSSIONS CONTINUED IN ADDITION TO LATER, PUBLICLY ANNOUNCED MEETINGS. DESPITE THE **TWO CHANNELS** OF DISCUSSION, UP TO THE TIME OF THE EASTER OFFENSIVE, **LITTLE PROGRESS** WAS MADE. THEN THREE THINGS HAPPENED IN 1972 THAT EASED THE **DEADLOCK.**

KISSINGER EMBARKED ON A **SECRET DIPLOMATIC EFFORT** THAT INCLUDED VISITS TO TOP LEADERS IN COMMUNIST CHINA AND THE SOVIET UNION, LONGTIME SUPPORTERS OF NORTH VIETNAM. THE MEETING AT BEIJING WAS PARTICULARLY IMPORTANT BECAUSE IT PAVED THE WAY FOR A **DIPLOMATIC COUP** THAT WOULD STUN THE WORLD.

ON FEBRUARY 21, 1972, PRESIDENT RICHARD NIXON MET CHAIRMAN MAO ZEDONG AND **REVERSED** 25 YEARS OF AMERICAN FOREIGN POLICY THAT HAD RECOGNIZED THE GOVERNMENT IN TAIWAN AS THE "ONLY" CHINA. HE ESTABLISHED RELATIONS THAT GAVE **FULL DIPLOMATIC RECOGNITION** TO THE **COMMUNIST** GOVERNMENT IN BEIJING AS THE ONLY **LEGITIMATE** CHINESE NATION.

NOT LONG AFTER, BEIJING PUBLICLY **MODERATED** ITS PROTESTS AGAINST AMERICAN ACTIONS IN VIETNAM. NIXON ALSO VISITED MOSCOW LATER THAT YEAR AND ACHIEVED **SIMILAR RESULTS** REGARDING THE SOVIET UNION'S POSITION WITH NORTH VIETNAM.

THE **THIRD EVENT** IN 1972 WAS THE FAILURE OF THE EASTER OFFENSIVE. IN AUGUST, NORTH VIETNAM'S HARD-LINE POSITION APPEARED TO **SOFTEN.** GENERAL TERMS FOR A **TRUCE** WERE AGREED UPON, WITH DETAILS TO BE WORKED OUT LATER.

ON OCTOBER 26, DR. KISSINGER RETURNED TO THE UNITED STATES AND **ANNOUNCED...**

WE BELIEVE THAT **PEACE** IS AT HAND.

1972 WAS AN ELECTION YEAR. NIXON WON IN A **LANDSLIDE.** HIS OPPONENT, **SENATOR GEORGE MCGOVERN** OF SOUTH DAKOTA, TOOK ONLY THE STATE OF MASSACHUSETTS AND WASHINGTON, D.C.

THE ELECTION BEHIND HIM, NIXON DEVOTED HIS ENERGIES TO BRINGING **CLOSURE** TO THE TRUCE NEGOTIATIONS. BUT PRESIDENT NGUYEN VAN THIEU OF SOUTH VIETNAM **BALKED** AT THE TERMS, PROTESTING THAT THEY WERE NOTHING MORE THAN **PAPER GUARANTEES** THAT THE COMMUNISTS WOULD **IGNORE** AT THEIR EARLIEST OPPORTUNITY.

NIXON GAVE THIEU **SECRET GUARANTEES** THAT HE WOULD SEND TROOP **REINFORCEMENTS** IF NORTH VIETNAM BROKE THE TRUCE. THEN THE COMMUNISTS **REVERSED** THEIR POSITION ON PREVIOUSLY AGREED UPON POINTS. THE PARIS PEACE TALKS HAD REACHED ANOTHER **STALEMATE.**

FURIOUS, PRESIDENT NIXON AUTHORIZED THE **MINING** OF NORTH VIETNAMESE **HARBORS** AND AN ALL-OUT **BOMBING CAMPAIGN** TO FORCE THE NORTH BACK TO THE **BARGAINING TABLE.**

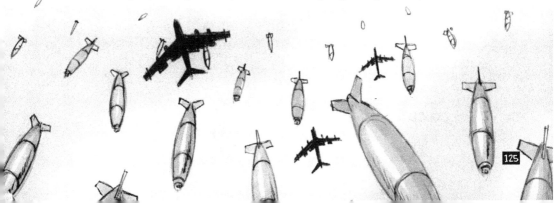

THE OPERATION WAS CODE-NAMED **LINEBACKER II.** BECAUSE IT TOOK PLACE AROUND THE HOLIDAY, THE U.S. PRESS CALLED IT THE **"CHRISTMAS BOMBINGS."** ON DECEMBER 28, 1972, THE NORTH VIETNAMESE DELEGATES AGREED TO MEET ONCE AGAIN TO DISCUSS TERMS.

ONE MONTH LATER, ON JANUARY 27, 1973, THE "AGREEMENT ON ENDING THE WAR AND RESTORING PEACE IN VIETNAM"--**THE PARIS PEACE ACCORDS**--WAS SIGNED BY DELEGATES FROM THE UNITED STATES, NORTH VIETNAM, SOUTH VIETNAM, AND THE VIETCONG.

ONE OF THE **TERMS** THAT ELICITED WIDESPREAD JOY AND **RELIEF** FOR AMERICANS WAS THE **RELEASE** OF AMERICAN PRISONERS OF WAR. AT LONG LAST, FOR THE UNITED STATES, THE WAR HAD **CONCLUDED.**

PART FIVE:
FORGETTING AND REMEMBERING

WHEN THE POWS RETURNED FROM **CAPTIVITY**, MANY AMERICANS BELIEVED THAT THE **WAR** IN VIETNAM WAS FINALLY **OVER**, AND THAT AT LONG LAST THEY COULD TURN AWAY, MOVE ON, AND **FORGET** THE CONFLICT.

THEY WERE **WRONG**.

AS PRESIDENT THIEU HAD PREDICTED, THE PARIS PEACE ACCORDS WERE QUICKLY **VIOLATED**--BUT BY BOTH NORTH **AND** SOUTH VIETNAM.

MEANWHILE, THE **DEPARTURE** OF THE LAST AMERICAN TROOPS FROM SOUTH VIETNAM **ACCELERATED**...

...AS DID THE **HANDOVER** OF ALL THE WEAPONS AND MATÉRIEL USED BY THE UNITED STATES DURING THE WAR. SOUTH VIETNAM'S ARMY WAS AS **WELL EQUIPPED** AS ITS COMMUNIST COUNTERPART.

BUT THIS **WEALTH** OF AMERICAN ARMS WAS **DECEPTIVE**. THE AMERICAN **ADVISORS** NEEDED TO INSTRUCT AND TRAIN THE SOUTH VIETNAMESE IN THEIR USE WERE **GONE**. BY THE END OF 1973, THERE WERE ONLY 50 AMERICAN SOLDIERS IN THE COUNTRY.

IN A MATTER OF WEEKS, THE **READINESS** OF THE SOUTH VIETNAMESE MILITARY BEGAN TO **ERODE**. AND BACK IN THE STATES, EVENTS UNFOLDED WITH IMPORTANT **CONSEQUENCES** FOR SOUTH VIETNAM.

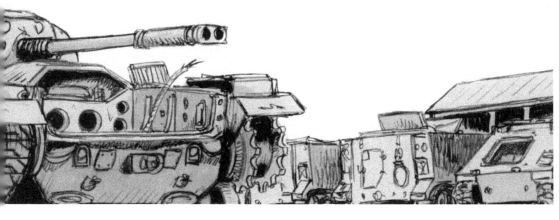

DURING THE 1972 PRESIDENTIAL CAMPAIGN, **BURGLARS** WERE ARRESTED ATTEMPTING TO BREAK INTO THE DEMOCRATIC NATIONAL COMMITTEE OFFICES IN THE **WATERGATE HOTEL**. IT WAS SOON REVEALED THAT THE BURGLARY WAS AUTHORIZED BY PRESIDENT NIXON. "WATERGATE" QUICKLY ENTERED THE **POLITICAL LEXICON** AS A NOUN FOR THE NIXON ADMINISTRATION'S WIDESPREAD **ABUSE OF POWER**.

DEMOCRATIC
NATIONAL
COMMITTEE

129

THOUGH THE GROWING **WATERGATE SCANDAL** DOMINATED THE NEWS, ANOTHER EVENT WITH IMPORTANT CONSEQUENCES OCCURRED IN WASHINGTON. CONGRESS, OVER PRESIDENT NIXON'S VETO, PASSED THE **WAR POWERS ACT** ON NOVEMBER 7, 1973.

IT PLACED **NEW LIMITS** ON PRESIDENTIAL WARMAKING POWERS AND ENSURED MORE **LEGISLATIVE CONTROL** OF THE NATION'S MILITARY. IT RENDERED NULL AND VOID PRESIDENT NIXON'S **GUARANTEE** TO PRESIDENT THIEU. CONGRESS ALSO **CUT FOREIGN AID** TO SOUTH VIETNAM. OUT OF $700 MILLION APPROPRIATED, ONLY $280 MILLION WAS DELIVERED.

THE WATERGATE SCANDAL FORCED PRESIDENT NIXON TO **RESIGN** IN DISGRACE ON AUGUST 9, 1974.

HE WAS SUCCEEDED BY **GERALD FORD**, WHO HAD BEEN THE REPUBLICAN **MINORITY LEADER** IN THE HOUSE AND APPOINTED TO BE NIXON'S VICE PRESIDENT IN DECEMBER 1973, TWO MONTHS AFTER **VICE PRESIDENT SPIRO AGNEW** WAS FORCED TO **RESIGN** OVER BRIBERY AND INCOME TAX EVASION CHARGES.

ON JANUARY 8, 1975, THE NORTH VIETNAMESE POLITBURO LAUNCHED **ANOTHER OFFENSIVE** TO "LIBERATE" SOUTH VIETNAM, CODE-NAMED THE **HO CHI MINH CAMPAIGN.** THE FINAL BATTLE FOR VIETNAM HAD BEGUN. WITH THE QUICK-VICTORY FAILURES OF THE TET AND EASTER OFFENSIVES IN MIND, THIS TIME THE POLITBURO PLANNED A **TWO-YEAR CAMPAIGN,** UTILIZING 20 DIVISIONS AND APPROXIMATELY 500,000 MEN.

AS IN THE EASTER OFFENSIVE, MANY SOUTH VIETNAMESE ARMY UNITS VALIANTLY **FOUGHT BACK,** WHILE OTHERS PANICKED AND FLED.

DUE TO THE **LIMITATIONS** OF THE WAR POWERS ACT, PRESIDENT FORD COULD NOT **HELP** SOUTH VIETNAM THE WAY NIXON HAD IN 1972. SOUTH VIETNAM WAS ON **ITS OWN.**

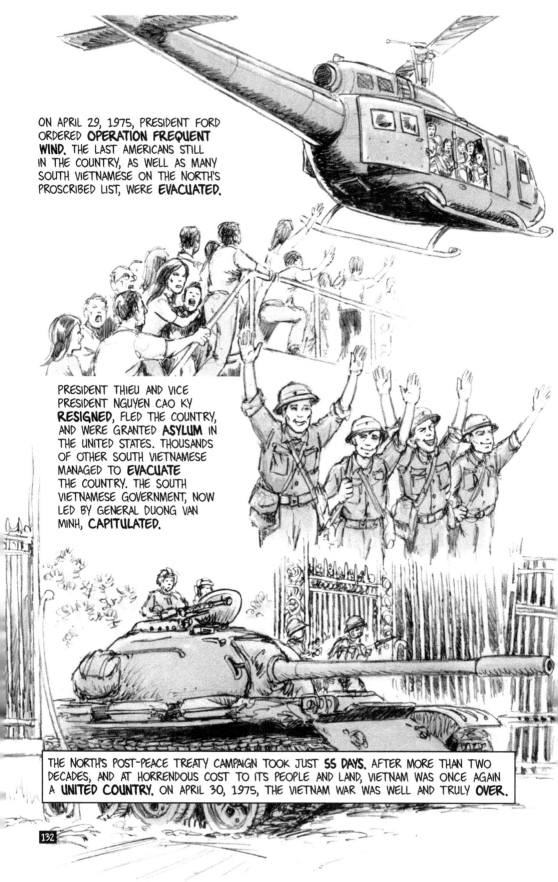

ON APRIL 29, 1975, PRESIDENT FORD ORDERED **OPERATION FREQUENT WIND.** THE LAST AMERICANS STILL IN THE COUNTRY, AS WELL AS MANY SOUTH VIETNAMESE ON THE NORTH'S PROSCRIBED LIST, WERE **EVACUATED.**

PRESIDENT THIEU AND VICE PRESIDENT NGUYEN CAO KY **RESIGNED,** FLED THE COUNTRY, AND WERE GRANTED **ASYLUM** IN THE UNITED STATES. THOUSANDS OF OTHER SOUTH VIETNAMESE MANAGED TO **EVACUATE** THE COUNTRY. THE SOUTH VIETNAMESE GOVERNMENT, NOW LED BY GENERAL DUONG VAN MINH, **CAPITULATED.**

THE NORTH'S POST-PEACE TREATY CAMPAIGN TOOK JUST **55 DAYS.** AFTER MORE THAN TWO DECADES, AND AT HORRENDOUS COST TO ITS PEOPLE AND LAND, VIETNAM WAS ONCE AGAIN A **UNITED COUNTRY.** ON APRIL 30, 1975, THE VIETNAM WAR WAS WELL AND TRULY **OVER.**

BUT THE END OF THE WAR DID NOT END THE **ANGUISH** IN THE UNITED STATES. ONE OF THE MOST CONTENTIOUS AND PAINFUL **LEGACIES** WAS THE FATE OF APPROXIMATELY 2,500 AMERICAN SERVICEMEN MISSING IN ACTION (MIA). EVEN THE NUMBER ITSELF REMAINS IN **DISPUTE.**

POW ★ MIA

THE NATIONAL LEAGUE OF FAMILIES OF AMERICAN PRISONERS AND MISSING IN SOUTHEAST ASIA WAS ORGANIZED TO HELP **FAMILIES** OF MIAs AND TO RAISE **AWARENESS.**

ALL 50 STATES NOW HAVE A **NATIONAL POW/MIA RECOGNITION DAY.** IN 1992, THE MIA ISSUE BECAME A PART OF THE **PRESIDENTIAL CAMPAIGN DEBATE** WHEN THIRD-PARTY CANDIDATE **ROSS PEROT** STATED HIS BELIEF THAT AMERICAN SERVICEMEN WERE STILL **ALIVE** AND BEING HELD IN VIETNAM AND REVEALED THAT HE HAD FUNDED **RETRIEVAL** EFFORTS.

YOU ARE NOT FORGOTTEN

OVER THE YEARS, PRIVATE ORGANIZATIONS AND GOVERNMENT-SPONSORED **SEARCHES** HAVE FOUND AND RETURNED THE REMAINS OF SOME MIAs. THE SEARCH **CONTINUES.**

AT FIRST, WHEN THE WAR ENDED, A **COLLECTIVE AMNESIA** APPEARED TO TAKE HOLD OF AMERICANS. FOR YEARS, IT SEEMED **NOBODY** WANTED TO REMEMBER ANYTHING ABOUT THE **WAR.**

THEN, IN 1979, A GROUP OF PEOPLE ORGANIZED THE **VIETNAM VETERANS MEMORIAL FUND.** THEY WANTED TO CREATE A MONUMENT TO HELP HEAL THE **EMOTIONAL SCARS** LEFT BY THE WAR. THE COST WAS ESTIMATED AT SIX TO TEN MILLION DOLLARS.

A **DESIGN COMPETITION** WAS HELD. EIGHT PEOPLE JUDGED THE ENTRIES AND MADE THE FINAL DECISION. A TOTAL OF 1,421 DESIGNS WERE SUBMITTED. ARCHITECT **MAYA YING LIN** WON WITH HER V-SHAPED BLACK GRANITE WALL LISTING THE NAMES OF ALL THOSE WHO HAD DIED IN THE WAR.

"THE WALL," AS IT CAME TO BE KNOWN, WAS **DEDICATED** ON NOVEMBER 11, 1982. MORE THAN 150,000 PEOPLE ATTENDED THE CEREMONIES, VETERANS AND RELATIVES OPENLY **WEEPING** WHEN THEY SAW THE NAME OF A FALLEN FRIEND OR FAMILY MEMBER.

FLOWERS, LETTERS, PHOTOS, AND OTHER **OBJECTS** LEFT BEHIND WERE GATHERED AND DISPLAYED ELSEWHERE BY THE NATIONAL PARK SERVICE--A **PRACTICE** THAT CONTINUES TO THIS DAY.

THERE WERE NUMEROUS **CRITICS** OF THE WALL'S DESIGN AND DEMANDS ROSE FOR A MORE **TRADITIONAL MEMORIAL.** TWO MORE MONUMENTS--STATUES--WERE ADDED NEARBY. THE FIRST WAS BY **FREDERICK HART,** WHO HAD PLACED THIRD IN THE ORIGINAL COMPETITION.

THE SECOND, THE **VIETNAM WOMEN'S MEMORIAL**, WAS BY GLENNA GOODACRE. IT MEMORIALIZES THE CONTRIBUTION OF THE 11,500 AMERICAN WOMEN WHO SERVED IN VIETNAM AS WELL AS THE EIGHT WHO DIED THERE.

THE WALL REMAINS A PLACE OF **PILGRIMAGE** AND REMEMBRANCE.

"At the Vietnam Wall"

because i never knew you
nor did you me
            i come

because you left behind mother,
        father and betrothed
and i wife and children
            i come

because love is stronger than enmity
and can bridge oceans
            i come

because you never return
and i do
            i come

DUONG TUONG
POEM LEFT AT THE BASE
OF THE WALL, 1995

POSTSCRIPT

THE VIETNAM WAR CAST A LARGE SHADOW THAT CONTINUES TO INFLUENCE AMERICAN CIVILIAN AND MILITARY THOUGHT AND CONDUCT. THE CLOSEST COMPARISON TO THIS EFFECT IS THE TRAUMA THE NATION SUFFERED DURING AND AFTER THE CIVIL WAR. RECOUNTING ALL THE VIETNAM WAR'S POST-CONFLICT INFLUENCES ON AMERICAN SOCIETY IS BEYOND THE SCOPE OF THIS VOLUME, AND WOULD MAKE FOR A SEPARATE GRAPHIC HISTORY IN ITS OWN RIGHT. BUT A FEW POINTS ARE WORTH NOTING HERE.

DOMINO THEORY

Arguably one of the most influential political theories to emerge from the cold war, it was a phrase first used by President Dwight Eisenhower in 1954 following the defeat of the French at Dien Bien Phu. This belief, that if one country fell to communism it would cause a chain reaction of communist takeovers of neighboring nations like a row of upright dominoes falling, would form the basis of American foreign policy worldwide for many years. Its most visible application was in Southeast Asia and the Vietnam War. While Laos and Cambodia, already destabilized by the conflict, did become communist, other nations did not--a fact that served to ultimately discredit the theory. Ironically, it was communist Vietnam that, in 1978, ousted the Cambodian communist government of Pol Pot and the Khmer Rouge because it threatened to destabilize the region. Political instability and violence continued to trouble Cambodia for more than two decades.

ANTIWAR MOVEMENT

The peak of the antiwar movement in America was reached in 1969 when a November march on Washington, D.C., attracted 500,000 protestors. But the gulf between young and old, conservative and liberal, a clean-cut business and middle-class culture and a counterculture that promoted a radically different appearance, drug use, and promiscuity, was too large for such a diverse range of society to remain united in purpose for long. The movement regained a measure of solidarity in 1970 following revelations of the My Lai massacre and the shooting of college student protestors on the Kent State University campus in Ohio by National Guardsmen, in which 4 students were killed and 16 wounded. With the end of the Vietnam War, some of its notable leaders took on new causes. Former SDS leader Tom Hayden entered California politics. Chicago Eight anarchist Abbie Hoffman remained on the fringe of society, and committed suicide in 1989. The Berrigan brothers continued their social activisim with the Plowshares Movement, formed in 1980.

THE CIVIL RIGHTS MOVEMENT

Social activism continued after the war and expanded to include other groups, both social and ethnic. Among them were the Hispanic El Movimiento and the American Indian Movement as well as the feminist and gay-and-lesbian communities. Over the years their social activism has inaugurated the passage of a number of laws that have struck down discriminatory policies. Though inequities still exist, the overall social standing of these groups and other minorities is significantly improved compared to conditions that existed in the 1960s.

U.S. MILITARY

The American military services all suffered enormously from the Vietnam War debacle. Plummeting morale, widespread drug abuse, budget cutbacks, social ostracism, and other ills plagued the branches for years following the end of the war. The nadir was reached when, in 1980, a joint-force special operations mission to rescue American hostages held in Tehran spectacularly failed-- exposing to the world America's military inadequacies. A massive turnaround was begun following the inauguration of President Ronald Reagan in 1981. Over the next two decades, numerous reforms were enacted, the most significant being the landmark Goldwater-Nichols Department of Defense Reorganization Act of 1986 and the Nunn-Cohen Amendment of 1987, which, among other things, established Special Operations as a separate command structure, administratively the equal of the traditional military branches.

WAR POWERS ACT

Also known as the War Powers Resolution, this law is still in effect and remains a controversial piece of legislation because it blurs the division of powers between the executive and legislative branches of government with respect to the declaration and conduct of war. It was invoked in 1982 when Marines were sent to restore peace in Lebanon; in 1993 to return American troops home after a failed peacekeeping effort in Somalia; in the Balkans during the civil war there in the 1990s; in 1990-91 for Operation Desert Shield/Desert Storm in Iraq; and following the terrorist attacks of September 11, 2001. Calls for its amendment or dissolution have occurred over the years, but political consensus has yet to reach the tipping point to put those words into action.

SUGGESTED READING

ACKNOWLEDGMENTS

SUGGESTED READING

BOOKS

APPY, CHRISTIAN G. **PATRIOTS: THE VIETNAM WAR REMEMBERED FROM ALL SIDES.** NEW YORK: VIKING, 2003.

CAPUTO, PHILIP. **A RUMOR OF WAR.** REV. ED. NEW YORK: HENRY HOLT AND COMPANY, 1996.

CLANCY, TOM, WITH FRANKS, FRED, JR., GEN. (RET.). **INTO THE STORM: A STUDY IN COMMAND.** NEW YORK: G. P. PUTNAM'S SONS, 1997.

CLANCY, TOM, WITH HORNER, CHUCK, GEN. (RET.). **EVERY MAN A TIGER: THE GULF WAR AIR CAMPAIGN.** NEW YORK: G. P. PUTNAM'S SONS, 1999.

CUTLER, THOMAS J., LT. CDR. **BROWN WATER, BLACK BERETS.** ANNAPOLIS, MD: BLUEJACKET BOOKS, 2000.

DAVIDSON, PHILLIP B. **VIETNAM AT WAR: THE HISTORY 1946-1975.** NEW YORK: OXFORD UNIVERSITY PRESS, 1991.

EDELMAN, BERNARD, ED. **DEAR AMERICA: LETTERS HOME FROM VIETNAM.** NEW YORK: W. W. NORTON & COMPANY, 2002.

HACKWORTH, DAVID H., COL. (RET.) AND SHERMAN, JULIE. **ABOUT FACE: THE ODYSSEY OF AN AMERICAN WARRIOR.** NEW YORK: SIMON & SCHUSTER, 1989.

HALBERSTAM, DAVID. **THE BEST AND THE BRIGHTEST.** REV. ED. NEW YORK: BALLANTINE BOOKS, 1992.

MCCAIN, JOHN, WITH SALTER, MARK. **FAITH OF MY FATHERS.** NEW YORK: RANDOM HOUSE, 1999.

MOORE, HAROLD G., LT. GEN. (RET.) AND GALLOWAY, JOSEPH L. **WE WERE SOLDIERS ONCE...AND YOUNG.** NEW YORK: HARPERPERENNIAL, 1993.

PROCHNAU, WILLIAM. **ONCE UPON A DISTANT WAR: DAVID HALBERSTAM, NEIL SHEEHAN, PETER ARNETT-- YOUNG WAR CORRESPONDENTS AND THEIR EARLY VIETNAM BATTLES.** NEW YORK: VINTAGE BOOKS, 1996.

SCHEMMER, BENJAMIN F. **THE RAID: THE SON TAY PRISON RESCUE MISSION.** NEW YORK: BALLANTINE BOOKS, 2002.

SHEEHAN, NEIL. **A BRIGHT SHINING LIE: JOHN PAUL VANN AND AMERICA IN VIETNAM.** NEW YORK: VINTAGE BOOKS, 1989.

SUMMERS, HARRY G., JR., COL. (RET.). **THE VIETNAM WAR ALMANAC.** NEW YORK: PRESIDIO PRESS, 1999.

WEST, BING. **THE VILLAGE.** NEW YORK: POCKET BOOKS, 2002.

YOUNG, MARILYN B. **THE VIETNAM WARS 1945-1990.** NEW YORK: HARPERPERENNIAL, 1991.

ZIMMERMAN, DWIGHT JON. **THE BOOK OF WAR.** NEW YORK: TESS PRESS, 2008.

-- -- --. **FIRST COMMAND: PATHS TO LEADERSHIP.** SAINT PETERSBURG, FL: VANDAMERE PRESS, 2006.

ZIMMERMAN, DWIGHT JON AND GRESHAM, JOHN D. **BEYOND HELL AND BACK: HOW AMERICA'S SPECIAL OPERATION FORCES BECAME THE WORLD'S GREATEST FIGHTING UNIT.** NEW YORK: ST. MARTIN'S PRESS, 2008.

ON THE INTERNET

AIR WAR COLLEGE DIGITAL LIBRARY
www.au.af.mil/au/awc/awcgate/awc-hist.htm#vietnam

BATTLEFIELD: VIETNAM
www.pbs.org/battlefieldvietnam

AMERICAN EXPERIENCE: VIETNAM ONLINE
www.pbs.org/wgbh/amex/vietnam

NAVAL HISTORICAL CENTER
www.history.navy.mil/wars/index.html

COMBINED ARMS RESEARCH LIBRARY DIGITAL ARCHIVE
cgsc.cdmhost.com

ACKNOWLEDGMENTS

I would like to thank General Chuck Horner for graciously taking time out of his busy schedule to contribute his foreword; my editor, Howard Zimmerman (no relation), whose advice and support on this project were invaluable; editor Thomas LeBien of Hill and Wang, without whom this project would never have happened; and most of all my wife, Joëlle, and daughter, Léa, who suffered through my "writing moods" during the creation of the script.

—Dwight Jon Zimmerman

I could not begin to list and/or point out all the sources, both textual and visual, that I have gathered together dealing with the Vietnam War in the past twenty-some-odd years. If I had to declare one significant reference, it would be my good friend Joe O'Donnell: his straightforward descriptions of experiences, events, and judgments (complete with color, smells, and sounds) taught me much about the 'Nam without my having to go there myself.

—Wayne Vansant

DWIGHT JON ZIMMERMAN is the author of *First Command: Paths to Leadership*. He has written on military subjects for American Heritage, the Naval Institute Press, *Vietnam* magazine, and the ongoing series of military-themed magazines about Special Operations and the U.S. Air Force, Navy, Army, Marine Corps, and Coast Guard for Faircount Publications. Zimmerman's essays for Faircount are now part of the curriculum of the Naval War College. He was the co-executive producer of the Discovery Channel's miniseries *First Command*, based on his book of the same name about American generals. Zimmerman had previously been an editor for Byron Preiss Visual Publications, and before that for Topps Comics and Marvel Comics, before leaving editing for writing.

WAYNE VANSANT was born in Atlanta, Georgia, in 1949. He served in the U.S. Navy during the Vietnam War, and graduated from the Atlanta College of Art in 1975. His first comic works appeared in Marvel's *Savage Tales*, and he was the principal artist for *The 'Nam* for more than fifty issues. He wrote and illustrated *Days of Darkness* for Apple Comics, telling the story of the early days of the war in the Pacific. The six issues were later published as a graphic novel. As well as doing work for Eclipse, Dark Horse, Byron Priess, and Caliber, he created a series of nonfiction military history comics called the Heritage Collection, which covered the Civil War and World War II. He lives in Powder Springs, Georgia.